GRAMOPHONE

EDITORIAL
Phone 020 7738 5454
email gramophone@markallengroup.com
EDITOR AND PUBLISHER Martin Cullingford
DEPUTY EDITOR Tim Parry
REVIEWS EDITOR Gavin Dixon
ONLINE CONTENT EDITOR James McCarthy
SUB-EDITOR David Threasher
SUB-EDITOR Marija Durić Speare
ART DIRECTOR Dinah Lone
'GRAMOPHONE PRESENTS ... MY CLASSICAL MUSIC' ART EDITOR Mary Holmes
PICTURE EDITOR Sunita Sharma-Gibson
AUDIO EDITOR Andrew Everard
EDITORIAL ADMINISTRATOR Libby McPhee
EDITOR-IN-CHIEF James Jolly
WITH THANKS TO Lucy Parry

ADVERTISING
Phone 020 7738 5454
email gramophone.ads@markallengroup.com
COMMERCIAL MANAGER
Esther Zuke / 020 7501 6368
SENIOR ACCOUNT MANAGER
James McMahon / 07967 169001

SUBSCRIPTIONS AND BACK ISSUES
0800 137201 **(UK)**
+44 (0)1722 716997 **(overseas)**
subscriptions@markallengroup.com

PUBLISHING
Phone 020 7738 5454
HEAD OF MARKETING
John Barnett / 020 7501 6233
GROUP INSTITUTIONAL SALES MANAGER
Jas Atwal
PRODUCTION DIRECTOR
Richard Hamshere / 01722 716997
PRODUCTION MANAGER Kyri Apostolou
CIRCULATION DIRECTOR
Sally Boettcher / 01722 716997
SUBSCRIPTIONS MANAGER
Bethany Foy / 01722 716997
EDITORIAL DIRECTOR Martin Cullingford
MANAGING DIRECTOR Paul Geoghegan
CHIEF EXECUTIVE OFFICER Ben Allen
CHAIRMAN Mark Allen

MA Music Leisure & Travel

Part of

Mark Allen

www.markallengroup.com

GRAMOPHONE is published by
MA Music Leisure & Travel Ltd, St Jude's Church,
Dulwich Road, London SE24 0PB, United Kingdom.
gramophone.co.uk
email **gramophone@markallengroup.com** or
subscriptions@markallengroup.com
ISSN 0017-310X.

recycle
When you have finished with
this magazine please recycle it.

**Founded in 1923 by Sir Compton Mackenzie and Christopher Stone as
'an organ of candid opinion for the numerous possessors of gramophones'**

Sharing so many musical journeys

Welcome to this special *Gramophone* publication, in which we've drawn together many of our most fascinating and thought-provoking My Music interviews from the past two decades. My Music has been a monthly feature in *Gramophone* since 2002, and it began with the simple idea of talking to a famous person outside of the world of classical music about its place in their life, and seeing where the conversation took us. Sometimes we'd discuss their favourite composers, or their first memories of listening to (or perhaps playing) music. Sometimes that person's profession would determine the topic – in the case of architects they might talk about building some of today's most admired concert halls, or in the case of actors the use of music in their films or plays. But more often than not, it has simply proven to be time set aside to share a personal passion, full of fond recollections and, just as importantly, recommendations. Reading through so many of the articles again in preparing this publication, two things struck me. The first is how, in so many cases, so many people's life-long love of classical music was started by someone who spotted an interest and took the time to nurture it, be it a teacher, a neighbour or a friend – something we can all play a part in. And secondly, that there is no single, let alone right, way to be a classical listener: audiences are as diverse as the music itself, a notion I know our partners on this publication, Classic FM, share and celebrate so wonderfully. We really hope you'll enjoy hearing from the huge variety of people who share their paths through their lives of listening every bit as much as we've enjoyed talking to them. And most of all, I hope they might inspire you to discover something new – be it work or composer – for yourself. Happy reading – and listening!

Martin Cullingford
Editor and

CLASSIC *f*M

It's a great delight and honour to partner with *Gramophone* for this very special My Classical Music edition. Over the three decades since Classic FM started broadcasting we've shared the greatest classical music across the UK with a mission to ensure that anyone and everyone can enjoy listening, regardless of background or previous classical musical knowledge. One of the many joys of my job is hearing from a listener who says they've just discovered Classic FM and are now tuning-in regularly, because they're hooked by the fantastic music we feature on a daily basis. So it's been a pleasure to help pick out the interviews contained within the following pages, with the many different stories of classical music discovery. I hope you enjoy reading the fascinating responses and that it inspires you to come and listen further to more of this wonderful music on Classic FM!

Philip Noyce
Managing Editor, Classic FM

GRAMOPHONE PRESENTS...
MY CLASSICAL MUSIC

Carlos Acosta

The ballet star, back in 2015, recalled learning to love classical music, as well as plans to re-create Bizet's Carmen for the Royal Ballet

My family wasn't from a classical background – we weren't considered cultural people. Another kid in my situation might have had a family member or a neighbour to point them in the right direction – to suggest books to read, music to listen to, museums to visit – but I didn't have that privilege. I didn't grow up with any exposure to classical music at all – I just assumed it was boring. Instead, I was surrounded by more popular trends – jazz, song, rhumba, salsa … and Michael Jackson! By the time I was nine, he was very famous; although American music was blocked from Cuba, people still managed to sneak it in.

My first introduction to classical was in ballet class, when the pianist would play music from operas or ballets. It was all new to me and it was only when I properly devoted myself to ballet at 13 that I started to love this music. At that point, I'd already been expelled from the National Ballet School of Cuba but then I saw a performance of *Flower Festival in Genzano*; I finally saw the purpose of what I'd been working towards. I wanted to do that, I wanted to jump like that. The dancers were very athletic, their bodies were so muscular, and I decided then and there to give it my best shot. Now that I've danced all the great ballets, the movement becomes an extension of the music. I know how to interpret it – where there is anger, passion, betrayal – and the movement reacts to the music.

I understand that some people can appreciate ballet music without the choreography. Tchaikovsky was an amazingly accomplished composer, and because he was so brilliant, his music stands alone. It's the same with Stravinsky's *The Rite of Spring*. But for me, I can't hear music like that without dancing to it. I went to the Proms recently and saw Leif Ove Andsnes play the Beethoven Piano Concertos Nos 1 and 4. Also on the programme was Stravinsky's *Apollon Musagète*, used for the ballet *Apollo*. Of course the tempos were quite different – nobody could dance that fast! – but still I couldn't stop moving. For dancers, when we learn the music, it's already married with the movement; it's very hard to separate the two.

I'm always trying to find out things about my own heritage and culture, and this led me to explore the music of Leo Brouwer. He's a wonderful Cuban composer and guitarist, and I began buying his music to see how I could use it in my own work. And with *Tocororo*, the ballet I created in 2003, I went to a composer-friend of mine, Miguel Núñez, and he gave me a selection of music that he'd composed but never used. From there, I could determine what I needed for my ballet – what music was going to accompany the love *pas de deux*, how the whole ballet would end … Sometimes I would re-edit what he gave me to suit the choreography – a similar process to my new ballet *Carmen* …

THE RECORD I COULDN'T LIVE WITHOUT

Massenet Manon
**Orchestra of the Royal Opera House /
Richard Bonynge** Decca
I still remember the last *Manon* I did – wonderful music, wonderful ballet, something I'll never forget!

We want to do our own thing, to put our own spin on Bizet's opera – I'm condensing the story to just three characters, Carmen, Escamillos and Don José – but at the same time I think there are ways to complement what Bizet did; you can add things without destroying the original concept. We're using the Shchedrin score as a base for something new – the conductor Martin Yates is providing original orchestration which will also feature voices (we'll have singers from the Royal Opera Chorus on stage during parts of the performance). I'm working with Martin on the score at the moment and it changes all the time, but we're determined not to spoil Bizet's wonderful tunes.

My listening habits have changed since growing up in Havana. I love opera – I've seen *Carmen* of course (I thought Jonas Kaufmann was brilliant as Don José) and a while back I saw Bellini's *La sonnambula* which had a Cuban, Eglise Gutiérrez, as Amina. She was unbelievable! There she was, a singer from a tiny city in Cuba, performing the title-role at the Royal Opera House! I was very proud. **G**

Tori Amos

Singer-songwriter Tori Amos travelled colourful byways en route to her classically inspired song-cycle, as she told us in 2011

I'd been playing the piano and composing since I was two-and-a-half when, at five, I was accepted into the Peabody Conservatory. I soon realised that my calling was to be a composer, but it was made very clear to me that this was a boys' club – you don't say Beethoven, Brahms, Amy Beach … This was the 1960s and women were burning their bras; I couldn't get into one, much less burn one, but I thought, 'I'm not going to play somebody else's music for the rest of my life'.

Before my mother married my father, a minister, she worked in a record store in North Carolina. Her tastes – Fats Waller, Cole Porter, all the musicals – and the pop music that my brother and sister would play all seeped in while I was at the Peabody.

It was tricky trying to negotiate my future. My father wanted me to be an organist and write church music but I thought that's as bad as going to a nunnery. I wanted to build sonic cathedrals of my own, from a woman's perspective. I pretty much got kicked out of the Peabody and, at 13, I turned pro and played clubs in Georgetown – my father chaperoned me. By 15 I was playing five nights a week in a Washington lobby bar – a mix of contemporary music and my own.

Then, at 21, I moved to LA, where I travelled away from the classical path. I'd been sending my own demos to record companies but, after seven years, I capitulated and opened myself up to a more commercial expression. If I had one more person knock over their beer on the piano at the Marriott, I was going to sling it in their face!

I did a bomb record with Atlantic and tried to get them to drop me, but they wouldn't. It took four years to develop *Little Earthquakes* and that's when I returned to the piano. *Night of Hunters* is my most classical project. When DG approached me last year and said, 'What about a 21st-century song-cycle based on classical themes?' I thought, 'Can I pick my head off the floor and then respond?' It's not a small task and if you get it wrong you get it really wrong. I'm aware of the purists who will think I'm touching a sacred thing, but I'm more interested in how the project will be viewed in a hundred years' time.

When I toured Europe last year I kept hearing stories about how people's lives had changed overnight. So I thought, if it's too loud, turn it up – let's do a song-cycle that starts at dusk and ends at dawn. Song-cycles work on the microcosm/macrocosm theory – so we have two people in a break-up and the 'Shattering' as he walks out, and then through the night there is this psychological process. Tori meets Annabelle, a shape-shifting creature of nature who encourages her to collect fragments from her past. My 12-year-old daughter, Natashya, sings Annabelle – she and I have this really creative relationship.

THE RECORD I COULDN'T LIVE WITHOUT

Schubert Winterreise

Dietrich Fischer-Dieskau *bar* **Gerald Moore** *pf*
DG

This was my guiding light. Without it, I wouldn't have agreed to *Night of Hunters*.

At the start, I said to the spirits of all the classical composers: 'If you want to be involved in this 21st-century expression, you'll show me'. Some – Mozart and Beethoven – were close by the whole time, but I couldn't make it work. Handel came close but Chopin stepped in at the final hour (in 'Cactus Practice') as did Debussy (in 'Carry'). Another guiding light was Stravinsky who pushed me to review his work. I listened endlessly to classical music, getting a sense of another sonic architect's way. When I was incorporating classical themes, it was the Schubert (in 'Star Whisperer') that came first. Once that nine-minute piece was locked in, the others began to flow.

With the Granados piece ('Fearlessness'), I thought the story would lead us to Spain but I got pushed by the piece for it to be on the water, and for it to go to the New World and then back to the Old World. I would argue with the Nine Muses, but they said: 'We're there for you, there are things you don't yet know'. I finished the piece and then found out that Granados had visited the New World and was on his way back to Spain when his boat went down. He was rescued, but he saw his wife drowning and in true fearlessness dove into the water. They both died. Ⓖ

'Night of Hunters' is available from DG

Adjoa Andoh

The actor - whose roles include Lady Danbury in Bridgerton - and director talked to us in 2022 about the music that inspires her

I can't remember a night when I was growing up when my dad didn't play his guitar and sing to my brother and I at bedtime. I remember having a friend for a sleepover once, and she looked at me like, 'What?' He'd play all sorts – folk, classical, calypso, The Chieftains, Harry Belafonte, Nat King Cole. And even once he'd said goodnight, he'd be noodling around on the harmonium downstairs, pedalling away furiously. He'll occasionally play it even now, and when he does I'm transported into being a little kid again, in bed and hearing this music wafting up the stairs.

My dad's mother had been a guitarist in a Palm Court Orchestra in the 1920s in Cape Coast, Ghana, and one of his earliest memories is of her playing the guitar to him dressed in a fabulous flapper outfit. My dad played the flute, mandolin and guitar, and had a beautiful tenor voice – he sang a lot of choral music (in fact, he still does). His brother was a musician, as was my brother (he and my nephew are now both musicians in America), and I used to play (terrible) second violin in the school orchestra, then cello in a jazz trio (I still play – very badly, very privately). So growing up in the Cotswolds, there was a lot of music – and music was music: it didn't matter whether it was traditional, *a cappella* or Bach.

There's an internal change when I listen to music. I notice it in my breathing, my focus, the clarity of my imagination. Whatever it is I'm working on at the time – if I'm writing, or even I'm just boiling some eggs – it allows me to be open, and enhances the reflective side of whatever I'm focusing on. I listen to a lovely new pianist called Hania Rani if I'm prepping for something – she records so that you can hear the action of the piano, and it's rather beautiful. And right now I'm listening to a lot of Sibelius. There's nothing particularly imaginative about my choices, I love *Finlandia* and the symphonies … And I always listen to a lot of Britten, *The Rite of Spring* – which I fell in love with at the age of 10 – and anything by Shostakovich: there's something hard won about his music, as if it comes out of a great deal of effort.

The composer Julie Cooper and I go back a long way. We did our first Equity job together in 1985 – we were in our early twenties, and ended up touring together for three years. We had come back together occasionally since then, but in January last year, by pure coincidence, she turned on BBC Radio 4 for the *Today* programme and heard *Moments of Light*, the piece I'd written about my reflection on lockdown and the light I'd found within the darkness. She got in touch and said, 'I'm composing my own musical response to the pandemic, an album "Continuum", and I think the opening piece would work really well with your words.' She sent me her draft version, and I began editing my piece, crafting it around the music I was hearing, trying to match the phrasing.

THE RECORD I COULDN'T LIVE WITHOUT

Holst The Planets
Berlin Philharmonic Orch / Herbert von Karajan
DG

I was filming *Invictus* with Clint Eastwood and Morgan Freeman in South Africa, and my eldest daughter and I sat in the Botanical Gardens and listened to the Cape Town Philharmonic play the whole suite as the sun was setting. It was amazing.

'Continuum' is available on various platforms, but I'm a vinyl girl myself. My brother and I would get up early on Sundays and put on Rimsky-Korsakov's *Sheherazade* – I still love that show-off thing where you drop the needle at the right point in the music. When I first encountered opera, 'Nessun Dorma' in the film *The Killing Fields*, I immediately tracked down the LP of *Turandot* at the library. When you get to know an opera, though, the arias you found fabulous are no longer as fabulous: you discover the less-popular ones, and how each one belongs.

The last opera I saw was *Peter Grimes* with Stuart Skelton. I was also at the Proms last year for *Hiawatha*; I'm very in love with Samuel Coleridge-Taylor, and I'm putting together a production celebrating his music at the Hackney Empire. I love live music-making. When I recorded drama for radio at Maida Vale, if the BBC SO were rehearsing I'd sneak into the gallery to watch. I love seeing sound being produced by an instrument: you hit it, you blow it, you pluck it and suddenly everyone's in this soul-soaring place. **G**

'Continuum' is available on Signum records

Simon Armitage

The poet in 2010 on being a chorister, Britten's songs, and listening to contemporary music

I remember the school orchestra, the music teacher attempting to shoehorn every kid in the class into some position in it. I was that classic novice who really worked his way down. I ended up with the triangle, and finally the wooden block.

There was quite a lot of classical music at home, and a recording of the *1812* Overture – I liked listening out for what I imagined to be the gun shots and the horses. Even though I thought classical music was difficult, if I thought there was a story behind it that made it much clearer and much more exciting.

For quite a long time I thought classical music was the enemy. I was of that classic punk generation; I really couldn't tolerate anything but very noisy, sloganeering punk rock. But then I did start listening again to classical music, and that coincided with the advent of compact disc. Maybe I was getting more interested in tonal ranges, and the idea of what sound could be. I particularly got into piano music at that time: Chopin, Shostakovich. I think there's something very intimate about the piano, particularly the piano on its own. I've realised of late that when I do turn to classical music I really want something quite dark, or solitary, or sorrowful. And Gregorian chant as well – I quite often have that playing in the background when I'm writing. I wonder if that appeals to the monk or the scribe in me.

I sing in a band, and I guess the notion that I can sing comes from being a chorister. I was head boy in the village choir for many years, and I will say immodestly that I had a very good voice, and it upsets me to wonder where that voice has gone. It was pretty much hymn-singing but occasionally the choirmaster would allocate solos. It was great when the vicar would say 'we'll now have hymn 364, and verse three will be sung solo by Simon Armitage'.

The last opera that I went to was *Peter Grimes* in Leeds, and it was absolutely astonishing. I hadn't seen it before and right from the very beginning I was on the edge of my seat. At the interval there were tears streaming down my face, I was so moved. Every musical phrase is very powerful and troubling – it's quite a disturbing event really. I've listened to quite a lot of Britten because he set a huge amount of poetry. Some of it works pretty well, some of it to my ears doesn't work at all. I think what happens is that poets write music into their poems – even if it's not metred there are often cadences and quite complex internal rhythms, and the minute you start to impose another rhythm on it things can go a bit haywire. It's a little bit easier I suppose with the Hardy poems he set, because a lot of the rhythms tend to be fairly regular so it's probably not that difficult to manoeuvre towards a musical end. But I've not been completely convinced by his Auden settings.

THE RECORD I COULDN'T LIVE WITHOUT

Ravel Music for piano
Werner Haas *pf* Philips/Decca
Ravel operates on the boundary of melody. Sometimes the music drifts beyond my understanding, then a really delicate, beautiful phrase drifts back in.

I wrote a libretto for an opera at the Edinburgh Festival, y the composer Stuart MacRae. His composition is, to my ears anyway, very avant-garde and contemporary. The actual performance was stunning. That's how I appreciated it, to think of it as an actual event – what you could see, what you could hear, what you could feel. That's been an experience that I've had quite a few times at the Contemporary Music Festival in Huddersfield. When I was younger I used to go along and sit there and listen and thought I don't find this very appealing at all, it doesn't make much sense to me as music. But I then stopped trying to interpret it in that way and just thought of it as an event. I got much more pleasure out of it then.

I'm writing an introduction for *Peter and the Wolf* for the Southbank; they're showing an animated film and wanted a different style of narrator. I'm writing a piece for this character who comes on to the stage and explains the role of the orchestra and the instruments. He's looking for a dream he had the previous night but has lost, which turns out to be *Peter and the Wolf*. **G**

Alexander Armstrong

From being a chorister to recording his debut album: the comedian, actor – and baritone – spoke to us in 2015 about his musical life

It's been a *wonderful* experience doing this album – an ambition ever since I left Cambridge, when I finally said goodbye, for the first time since the age of 11, to full-time choral commitment. That was something at the time I thought I did very lightly, but I didn't, because I've been hidebound by it, and my conscience has over the years weighed incredibly heavily in terms of my absence from classical music.

My recurring nightmare is of turning up to choir practice having not been there for years, to find my cassock – which I can see will now be slightly tight around the middle – hanging rather glumly in the corner, and everyone having to find music for me – though all being nice enough not to ask where the hell I've been. This is what comes back to haunt me.

At my first school the choir was run by the headmaster's wife – an enormously influential character, a sort of mother to all the boys. These were unbroken boys' voices obviously, so the bass part was sung up an octave, but she would play around with things so it wasn't too bad. But it was very high quality. I remember going to hear the Vienna Boys' Choir singing at Hexham Abbey and being really very disappointed, and thinking, 'They might be famous but they're not a patch on us!'

Then she and the headmaster split up – we came back from Christmas, and she'd gone. My mother scouted around to find something to keep my interest going so I became a chorister at St Mary's Cathedral in Edinburgh. I'm devoted to Choral Evensong. I find the liturgy so beautiful, but it's not just the sound of a Precentor singing 'Lighten our darkness, we beseech thee, O Lord' at that lovely, shadowy time of the day (with the sound of distant traffic, where an inner-city cathedral becomes a wonderful sanctum within a busy town or city), it's also the settings of the Canticles, and a really well-sung Psalm – it's just such a part of me, I adore it.

Richard Marlow, who was Director of Music at Trinity College, remains such a hero of mine. The descants he wrote for carols and hymns are some of the most exquisite – so ornate, but clever. What a brilliant man. It was lovely to spend really good, intense time under his instruction. I remember thinking, 'Golly, I'll never sing in a choir like this again!'

When I first left Trinity I used to dep at St Paul's Knightsbridge, where my old friend James Morgan was the choirmaster. But then I stopped. I used to do a comedy club on Saturday nights, and although the St Paul's Eucharist is at 11 o'clock, we'd have to be in at 10. And quite often you'd be the only bass on your side, and you'd be singing a full Palestrina Mass that you perhaps didn't know as well as you might have hoped … and you might rather wish that you hadn't been up until half-past-three or four in the morning.

THE RECORD I COULDN'T LIVE WITHOUT

Bach St Matthew Passion
Sols; Monteverdi Choir; English Baroque Soloists /
John Eliot Gardiner DG Archiv
There's a lovely inherent jazziness, little rhythms, and eddies and flows that I find so poetic.

The two lives weren't enormously compatible, so very sadly I let that go. I suspect that's when the dreams started.

For years, ever since I started in acting, I'd say, 'But I sing as well', and they'd said, 'Yeah, yeah … just read from the top of page three'. But what I *really* meant is that all my life I've been singing, and I'm trained. I don't think anybody ever really believed it – it would be like someone coming in and saying, 'Oh, and I can ride horses too' … 'Yes, yes, yes, we can all ride horses.' It's just one of those things that everybody has on their CV. Clean driving licence. Can sing. Then I was doing an interview on Steve Wright's show on BBC Radio 2 four years ago, and someone said, 'Tell us something surprising about yourself', and I said, 'Well I'm a trained classical baritone' – and he said, 'Nonsense!' and I said, 'Genuinely, genuinely!' So I got to sing in a few things, and eventually – it's only taken 25 years – somebody said, 'Oh, I see what you mean, oh you sing *properly*', so I've been given a leg up. Ⓖ
Armstrong's 'A Year Of Songs' is available on East West Records

Music Classical

Download the app

Justice Ruth Bader Ginsburg

Only the second woman to be appointed to the US Supreme Court, in 2019 the liberal icon discussed opera, equality, and her eponymous album

It all started with Dean Dixon, a conductor who was on a mission to turn children on to classical music and took mini operas to all the schools in New York City. I grew up in Brooklyn and when I was 11 my teacher took me to a high school where they were putting on an abbreviated version of Ponchielli's *La Gioconda*. I'd played the piano since I was eight years old, and in ninth grade I'd taken up the cello, but opera was new to me. And I'd never seen anything like it – the glorious music, the drama! This was in 1944. Five years later Dixon left the US, saying: 'In all the time I've been conducting here, no one has ever called me "Maestro".' And that was because he was an African-American. He went to Europe and had a flourishing career, and when he returned to the US, every major orchestra wanted him. It's a good illustration of how US society had changed over those years.

So I started to go to the opera. When my late husband was stationed in Oklahoma, the Met toured to Dallas, Texas, and I saw Zinka Milanov, my first Tosca. And when we were in Harvard, we'd see the Met when it came to Boston; I recall a *Butterfly* with the soprano Antonietta Stella – it was directed by a Japanese director, and Stella moved like a Japanese woman. When we moved to New York, we got a subscription to the Met, and we kept it going when the Company moved to Lincoln Center. There was a marvellous production of Barber's *Anthony and Cleopatra* in 1966, and the stage design meant that anything that could go wrong *did* go wrong. Meanwhile, across the way in the State Theater was a smaller production by New York City Opera of Handel's *Julius Caesar* with Beverly Sills as Cleopatra and Norman Treigle as Caesar. It was magical. I loved Sills. For a long time she sang at City Opera – it was only much later that she finally sang at the Met.

In my younger days, I never saw an opera where an orchestra had female players. Then someone had the bright idea to drop a curtain between those auditioning and the panel, and things changed overnight. I wish we could have a drop curtain in every field of human endeavour.

And now we're seeing female opera directors, too. I moved to DC in 1980 and over the years I've watched the Washington National Opera get better and better. Francesca Zambello, the artistic director, is tremendous, and they have a very good Young Artist Program; I took my Chambers staff to its annual showcase, a performance of *La traviata*, in October.

I live next door to Kennedy Center so I like going to recitals there as well as opera (even though I try not to go out when Court is in session – sometimes I'll bring my law books with me). It's a chance to pause, to just enjoy the music. There was a recital recently by the bass-baritone Ryan Speedo Green, who had a book, *Sing for Your Life*, written about him.

THE RECORD I COULDN'T LIVE WITHOUT

'Notorious RBG in Song'

Patrice Michaels sop Kuang-Hao Huang pf Cedille

The CD is based on my own life, but it's a family affair. My daughter-in-law wrote the song-cycle and performs the whole disc, and my son produced it.

He lived in a poor neighbourhood, had a dysfunctional family and got into trouble at school, but a teacher took him to the Met to see Denyce Graves in *Carmen* and he said: 'I'm going to sing there one day.' He ended up winning the Metropolitan Opera National Council Auditions in 2011. I tried to get him to give a concert at Court, but he was under contract with the Vienna State Opera at the time and couldn't be released.

The 'Notorious RBG in Song' CD started with 'Anita's Story'. Anita was my husband's secretary and a few years ago I found a letter she wrote to me about how she became a feminist through typing up my briefs; my son and daughter commissioned songs from three female composers for my 80th birthday, and this was used for one of them, set by my wonderful daughter-in-law, the soprano Patrice Michaels. Then Patrice composed a whole song-cycle around it, and *The Long View* is the result. Stacy Garrop was another of the female composers who was approached for my 80th; after my husband died, I found in a drawer a most beautiful love letter he had written and this is what Stacy based her song on. It was essential that we include this on the recording – he was so important in my life and in the lives of our children. **G**

Alec Baldwin

The actor, in 2009, on his dream job –
presenting a classical music radio show

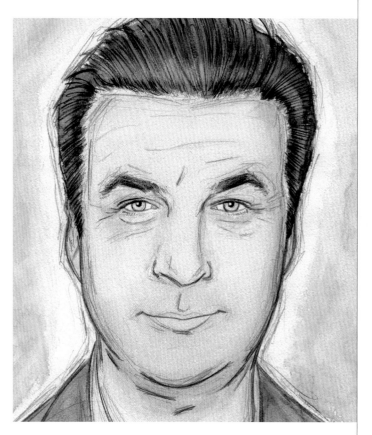

I didn't fall in love with classical music until I was an adult. I had heard it as a child in school – back then, there was still exposure to classical music, even in a limited way, in the school system – but it didn't really do anything for me. It took me until much later to discover this entire, rich universe of music that now I really can't live without.

In 1982 I was working on a television show, a soap opera called *The Doctors*. They cued in Berlioz's *Symphonie fantastique*. I turned to the casting director, Roger Sturtevant, and I asked him, 'What music is that?' He looked at me really scornfully as if he couldn't believe I didn't know it already. I felt so stupid! So unfortunately, that first real experience for me was coloured by the arrogance that makes classical music so forbidding to lots of people, the 'how can you not already know all of this?' pompousness.

Even so, I managed to find my way in, and classical music became an insatiable craving for me. I loathe and detest most pop music, and living in Los Angeles in the 1980s meant I spent a great deal of time in isolation, driving in my car to this appointment and that. So it was in my car that I gained my musical education, listening to classical radio stations. I've become the kind of person who shows up late to appointments because I can't bear to turn off the car radio until I've heard the whole piece. For years, back in the days of car phones, I had the phone in my car programmed to speed-dial various classical music stations, so that I could ask them exactly what it was that I was just listening to, with all the recording information.

In all the travel I do these days, I still constantly comb the dial to find the local classical music station. Now, in the US, there are so many locations that don't have any radio stations dedicated to classical music, not even the public radio stations.

From that first piece, *Symphonie fantastique*, I moved to Tchaikovsky and Rachmaninov, pieces like the *Pathétique* Symphony and *The Isle of the Dead*. I still adore Romantic music, although within a few years of that discovery of Berlioz, I'd begun listening to Bach and Beethoven and many of the earlier masters.

However, Mahler is a great, great love of mine. The recent entire Mahler cycle at Carnegie Hall, with Pierre Boulez and Daniel Barenboim splitting the conducting between them with the Staatskapelle Berlin, was momentous.

Over time, I began to develop a real fetish for hearing certain composers with very specific conductors and orchestras. I craved Leonard Slatkin conducting Copland, Falla's *Three-Cornered Hat* conducted by Eduardo Mata, the Montreal

THE RECORD I COULDN'T LIVE WITHOUT

Mahler's Symphony No 9
Chicago SO / Sir Georg Solti Decca
I love the power, the searing quality, of Mahler, in all of his symphonies but especially in this one. The whole universe of emotion is contained in this piece.

Symphony and Charles Dutoit doing Rachmaninov and Tchaikovsky. I fell in love with Sir Georg Solti and the Chicago Symphony.

Our country could use its own soundtrack, our own musical narrative, right about now. I'd suggest Holst's *The Planets*. We've so completely obliterated our own landscape, and so completely embraced corporate identities rather than finding our own values, that we're going to need to go to a different planet and start over.

I've often thought that if I weren't acting, I'd really like to be a classical radio programme host. How much fun would that be! What I would play would depend on the time of day I was on. For the daytime? Copland, Wagner, Falla. For night, Mahler of course, but also a lot of piano music: Ravel, Rachmaninov, Debussy, Chopin, Satie. Someone at the New York Philharmonic read an interview with me in which I mentioned that idea a while back, and so now I am involved in classical music radio: starting this fall, I'm hosting the orchestra's weekly radio broadcasts, which is an amazing honour. ⒢

ILLUSTRATION: KEVIN SPENCER

Ed Balls

The Labour politician in 2015 on learning the piano while being Shadow Chancellor, and the terror of performing Schumann in concert

My parents met in a church choir in Norwich when they were 15, and singing in choirs was something they've done throughout their adult lives. So from the earliest I can remember there was music in the house, particularly choral music; I probably knew the key bits of *Messiah* and *Zadok the Priest* before I could really remember anything else.

I went to Keble College, Oxford, which then, as now, had a strong Anglican music tradition. During my time there, I heard the music of Howells for the first time, which has been a big thing for me ever since. It's not very often in music that you can say the 20th century was *the* century – but in Anglican cathedral music it was brilliant. When I was Secretary of State for Children, Schools and Families, my office was opposite Westminster Abbey, which held a service for the department. I was allowed to choose the music, so I chose Dyson in D.

I started to play the violin from the age of seven, and played for about 15 years. I do have very good memories, though some bad ones too – in the school orchestra I scrubbed my way through a lot of operatic overtures and symphonies, which I didn't particularly enjoy. But I had a very good violin teacher who also played semi-professionally, and so we played a lot of Handel *concerti grossi* and a bit of *The Four Seasons*, and when I was 14 we did a performance of *The Lark Ascending* in which he played the solo part – there was no way I could get anywhere near to playing that, but I could play the second violin part in the orchestra, and the piece has remained one of my favourites.

The reality is that I liked playing music with other people, but was never really good enough to play on my own – that's the tragedy of the violin. A couple of times I played in quartets – 15 years ago I played in a string quartet with John Gapper and Gillian Tett, now top columnists for the *FT*. But I stopped doing that kind of thing for a long time – until I started playing the piano.

I started lessons just as I became Shadow Chancellor, in January 2011. I decided that, if I was going to do it, the only way to learn properly was to do the exams – to make myself play the scales and learn the techniques. I took Grade 1 that November. It was like being nine years old again – there was no concession to the fact that I was an adult. Afterwards I lent over to the examiner and said, 'It's much more stressful than the House of Commons' – and realised from his expression that you're not meant to have a conversation! We established a rule early on at home: when I start a new grade and choose my three pieces, I have to get the agreement of all the family on them – and Yvette has a veto – because they are going to hear them lots and lots of times…

THE RECORD I COULDN'T LIVE WITHOUT

Handel Ariodante – Dopo notte
Dame Janet Baker *mez* ECO / Raymond Leppard
Decca

When I went to my interviews for university and work, this was the tape on my headphones that I'd listen to on the way there. It's something I associate with leaving home and with doing new things.

The Editor of *The Guardian*, Alan Rusbridger, asked me to take part in a concert in which different people played one of the 13 pieces of Schumann's *Kinderszenen*. It was on a Sunday morning the weekend after the Autumn Statement. I did a little bit of practice at 9am, then went and did the Murnaghan programme on Sky live at 10am, and then went back for the concert. I played the final piece, the reflective meditation on childhood, which from my point of view meant it was the slowest. But then you walk out, and you suddenly realise there are 500 people out there, and it's utterly quiet … My hands were really shaking, but I managed to get through it without making a mistake. But it was so difficult! The TV and politics were nothing compared to this.

I've since played the Schumann live on Jeremy Vine's programme, with seven million people listening to me. I've had so many letters from people I've never met, all writing about how they've started to play the piano in their fifties, sixties and seventies. These days when I get into a black cab, the driver won't say anything about politics – they'll turn round and say, 'How's the piano going?' **G**

Tony Banks

The Genesis keyboardist talked to us in 2004 about composing his orchestral suite, Seven

My mother was musical – she had a very good piano technique – but she did need the music in front of her. I didn't. Or at least I wasn't a natural at reading music; I was better at picking up things by ear. My father was tone-deaf. When I was 13 or 14 I'd play the piano all day every day, but the prospect of music as a career was just a fantasy.

By 1963 The Beatles were breaking through and everybody wanted to be in a band, even if not everybody expected you to be – especially if you were at Charterhouse School. It wasn't the done thing. In fact we weren't allowed radios or gramophones in the school! But it was there that I met Peter Gabriel and our musical tastes started to develop together – we got heavily into American soul, the Beach Boys, Jimi Hendrix, quite a mix. We would write songs together with another student, Mike Rutherford.

It was seeing The Nice at the Marquis Club in London, one of the most exciting experiences of my life, that got me thinking about performing live. So having spent a year at university (I was reading chemistry and then logic with physics) we decided instead to form Genesis. Our first single, *The Silent Sun*, deliberately sounded like the Bee Gees but we wanted to be more than just a pop band. The live element of Genesis was always interesting, even if it wasn't always planned: Peter would often surprise us with his costumes but it got us noticed. We were occasionally accused of being a Glam Rock band, but that wasn't us at all. The visuals were always just a way of interpreting the music, of adding atmosphere, of telling stories.

From our early days we liked the extended song, so the idea of doing a connected album, a 'songcycle' – 'The Lamb Lies Down on Broadway' – was very appealing and it became a sort of signature album for us. The label that did stick to us was 'Progressive' and if that means trying to do things that hadn't been done before, then, yes, we were a Progressive Rock band. But we were different from bands like Yes or Pink Floyd.

There were other musical references, too: I love Ravel's strong melodies and his use of unusual notes in compound chords, not so much the style, more the pianistic effect of it. The opening of *Daphnis and Chloe* – something repetitive that rises up to a big release with a key change at the top of the build – appeals enormously. Harmony is where I start when I write – I think chords upwards.

Stravinsky doesn't excite me much, but I do love *The Rite of Spring* – those bold rhythmic brass phrases! – and our guitarist, Steve Hackett, liked Albinoni, Satie and classical guitar and he brought a more specifically classical edge to the band. 'Classical' is a funny word – to me it's Beethoven, it's back in time – that's

THE RECORD I COULDN'T LIVE WITHOUT

Martinů Symphony No 4. Memorial to Lidice.
Czech PO / Jiří Belohlavek
Chandos

Martinů probably suffered from being too prolific, but I love the wild things he does with his chords, particularly in the Fourth Symphony - the fast second movement is particularly effective in its control of the strong rhythms that pulse through it. Equally, the Memorial to Lidice, which is so simple in the way it builds up (albeit with a slightly embarassing quote at the end from Beethoven's Fifth) that it's difficult not to admire it.

why I call *Seven* an orchestral work. The kind of music I write is quite rich harmonically, and allows me to go places. I wanted to do a totally pure thing, nothing hybrid, no synthetic instruments, with a palette developed over centuries and with a lovely combination of sounds. I love the sound of choirs for that reason, too, although I have a problem with the operatic style of singing, that very tutored voice, the heavy vibrato that *used* to be the rule.

Seven's influences are largely 20th-century British – Vaughan Williams, the archetypal English composer; Elgar because he's so strong melodically; Delius because he's capable of building such strong atmospheres. I can see definite influences in the second part of *Seven*, but I hope it's less obvious elsewhere. It surprised me how accessible it sounded. The strong themes which I build to, do deliver. I'm trying to build everything to send a shiver down the spine. **G**

Tony Bank's 'Seven' is available on Naxos

ILLUSTRATION: NEALE OSBORNE

John Barry

The film composer, who died in 2011, spoke to us in 2006 about the place of music in his life, from childhood memories onwards

Music of many types surrounded me as I grew up in York. My father owned a group of theatres in Lancashire and Yorkshire. The main one was also a concert hall which played host to a wide range of acts, from the Philadelphia Orchestra to Nat King Cole.

Many times, the stars from abroad would play big dates in London and Glasgow or Edinburgh, so they would stop off en route at my father's concert hall. I loved all of this, and used to get them to sign my programmes. I've still got many of them. When the artists left, I used to go to the train station and see them off with my dad. There was a practical reason for us being there, too. Sometimes they would be running late, and dad would negotiate with the platform keeper to hold up the trains.

Not only did I get to witness all of these great concerts, but often the stars would come to our house for dinner. I didn't talk to them very much, having to be on my best behaviour, but some of them became close family friends. John Barbirolli and his wife Evelyn Rothwell came with the Hallé Orchestra nearly every May for several years. He was such an inspiration and infused me with a great and deep love of music. He would tell me stories or play the cello for us. He made such an impression on me. I've since amassed a huge collection of classical scores.

The first music I really loved was Chopin's piano music. I never knew why at the time, but now I see that it was very melodic, in almost songlike style. I suppose I got to know Chopin through the 1945 movie *A Song to Remember*, with Cornel Wilde as Chopin bleeding all over the piano keys – that had a great effect on me.

Films in general were an enormous part of my musical education, so it's unsurprising that I became a movie composer. When I used to go to the afternoon show at the cinema and hear all of those scores by greats like Max Styner, I would hear something I liked – a scene with a clever musical idea – and make a mental note. I'd go back to the evening show and see it again. Then I'd rush out and buy the records.

I didn't realise it at the time, but I was getting the best kind of musical education. And much of it was classical. Film scores were being written by Shostakovich and Prokofiev. Prokofiev's soundtrack for Eisenstein's film *Alexander Nevsky* blew me away.

Similarly, when I listened to Chopin I used to get ideas and would write maybe four or eight bars. Those small snatches would stand me in good stead when I became familiar with the 32-bar traditional song form, a structure that has incredibly never worn thin and still works today.

THE RECORD I COULDN'T LIVE WITHOUT

Stravinsky The Rite of Spring
Kirov Orchestra / Valery Gergiev
The work featured in Disney's film *Fantasia*, which I saw as a youngster. Here was a brilliant movie score that wasn't actually a movie score!

I've never divided music. I have very broad tastes and that love for many styles served me well with scoring for movies. Across the 11 James Bond movies I scored, for instance, I tried to stretch the genre's boundaries a bit. It was like scoring the same movie 11 times! It was a formula. So it was like variations on a theme. *You Only Live Twice* was very lush, very romantic and in some ways indebted to my love for the Russian composers.

Prokofiev and Shostakovich did movie scores, in the right way. They didn't just write music, they wrote theatre. They knew about composing for theatre and ballet, so it was all very dramatic, bound up with the story. I look at some movie composers now and wonder where on earth their ideas have come from. You need to know where in the film the musical thought comes from. Personally, I work with a main theme first that captures the characters or the situation and then work outwards.

Some classical composers look down upon film musicians as something rather dreadful. They see films as trite. That's their problem. I love the combination of the visual and musical elements. That tight control, the 24 frames a second you have to work with and the ways you can have very flowing melodies within that, are what make the score sound complete, if you use the form properly. ⓖ

Simon Russell Beale

The actor spoke to us in 2007 about his musical loves – particuarly Beeethoven

It was dad who brought music to my life. He was a chorister at St Paul's, so it was only natural that I was sent there as well, when I'd just turned eight. And that was my job from then until I reached my early 20s. All of the choristers went on to be music scholars; the headmaster told us that was expected. So I sang a service every day of my life for years.

All of my chorister friends auditioned for the London music colleges and I got a place at the Guildhall on the singing course. But I wasn't good enough, and rather lazy. Somewhere in the back of my mind I knew that drama was my real interest, so I changed to acting.

Surprisingly, given my love of theatre and music, I'm not an opera freak. My little brother Matthew Beale is an opera singer (he sang Don Ottavio for Welsh National Opera recently) and ironically he's the only one of us who grew up without any musical training! I would like to direct opera, because I'm interested in the problems that singers traditionally have with acting. I mean, what the hell do you do with a long Handel aria? But also more basic things. Watching Matt work in that world, I've noticed that singers like him or Simon Keenlyside (with whom I was at university; we even sang together once) have a different attitude and take the acting extremely seriously, so I think there's great potential there.

Nineteenth-century German symphonic repertoire is the area that really draws me in. When I was about 13, I was out driving with my father when he played the beginning of Mahler's Eighth Symphony. It was incredibly impressive, huge, exciting, and that was the first mini-score I bought. I wanted to see what something so massive looked like. It was terribly expensive; all my pocket money went into buying it. Rather sentimentally I kept it for years and then sadly lost it.

About five years ago I rediscovered Beethoven. As a student, my head of music had once said to me: 'I wish you didn't have to listen to Beethoven until you were older.' I didn't know what he meant. I had anyway done the Seventh Symphony for A-Level, and just thought, 'Yeah, yeah, Beethoven is fine but not nearly as interesting as Stravinsky'. But all those years later I started listening to him again properly and realised that he is truly brilliant and his symphonies are perfect.

Consequently that area of interest was inflamed, and I got into Brahms and Schubert again, then Bruckner and back to Mahler. I find the whole idea of the pressure of Beethoven's time and the years after him just fascinating … the idea of these other poor sods having to write their symphonies under the giant shadow of Beethoven. It is actually so moving to think how they managed to cope with it, with that immense pressure.

THE RECORD I COULDN'T LIVE WITHOUT

Bach Mass in B minor
Ensemble Vocal de Lausanne / Michel Corboz
Erato
If I had to die with one piece of music playing, this would be it. It's a perfect piece.

The Beethoven symphony I find almost impossible to grasp is the Ninth. I just don't know where to pin my brain. It is supposed to express joy, and he shoves his singers up to the highest imaginable tessitura. They sound uncomfortable, and that, along with other questions, such as why the Turkish march is there and why he uses voices in the first place – puzzles me. I've done a fair amount of singing on stage, not least in musicals like Bernstein's *Candide* and now *Spamalot*. I found it less anxious than I expected, I suppose because it was part of a different process – the singing itself wasn't the main reason for me being there. I'd love to do some Sondheim. I am an enormous fan of his. I've got my eyes set on *Into the Woods* one day, and perhaps *Sweeney Todd*.

I've just narrated a disc of Benjamin Britten's film scores. It was nostalgic for me because we used to see the film *Night Mail* at school every year as part of the Christmas film showings. Those long passages are hard, it's difficult to know where to breathe. I don't know how the original narrator did it, it goes on for pages. Only the fact that it's great writing by Auden carries you through, but even so I had to go back to re-record a bit.

The benchmark recording for me when I was at school, though, was Neville Marriner's performance of Handel's *Messiah*. I was 14 and was hit by his lightness of touch and speed. That's when I got the early music bug. **ⓖ**

John Bird

The founder of The Big Issue talked to us in 2014 about discovering music, weekly trips to Wigmore Hall, and the joy of singing

My father, even though he was a builder's labourer, was obsessed with Caruso, and I inherited that. We were always listening to Caruso on a Sunday morning as the dinner was being made. I always remember that and it's incredible that my father should have been so aware of the power of the human voice.

When I was in a boys' prison they used to let us out and we'd go to see the local Guildford Municipal Orchestra, and everybody else was there because it gave them a chance to look at girls, but I was there riveted by, obsessed by, the music. I'm a BBC Radio 3 man, and when I later worked in factories as a printer we used to have these arguments as to whether we listened to Radios 1, 2 or 3 – and I always won. So in the course of the working day I would have more hours listening to Radio 3 than they would get, and I would lecture them and say that the music they wanted to listen to was a corruption of their mind, body and ears! And eventually I won some of them over.

When I was in my late thirties I decided to become a mature student, and one of the subjects I went to study was Music, at a place called the Ealing College of Higher Education – now it's part of the University of West London. There was a guy who taught music called Christopher Small, who died recently, and it was a brilliant course. The aim wasn't to try to turn people into musicologists – it was just to lift your cultural soul. I had a brilliant time. That's where I discovered Liszt.

For three years I lived around the corner from Wigmore Hall in Marylebone and I'd go to concerts every week. I'd given up drinking, smoking and chasing women – and I had to fill my time! So I would do that by going to the Wigmore. I wanted to participate in this art form – where so much discipline, so much effort and so much refining had been put in to it. That's the staggering thing about live music. I miss that now. I do occasionally go to things in Cambridge, but not as much as I used to. We can always pop up to Ely, too. I recently went into the Lady Chapel in Ely Cathedral, just by happenstance, and I soon had my whole family watching a workshop of four or five cellos. It was absolutely riveting.

I'm not scientific about my appetite. I've been listening to a lot of Rachmaninov and I'm interested in people like Hindemith, people who are kind of off the radar. I like atonality and I like Webern's music, and I got into that largely through the filter of Liszt. Someone once said to me, 'you're listening to Liszt, what's he like?' And I said that he's like a man playing with his elbow. I'm a devotee, not an aficionado – I just love classical music. I'm obsessed. I always feel an enormous regret every year that because of

THE RECORD I COULDN'T LIVE WITHOUT

Ravel Boléro (arr for two pianos)
Katia and Marielle Labèque *pfs*
KML Recordings
When played on two pianos *Boléro* is brilliant, like it has been stripped down to the bare bones.

my schedule I never get to the BBC Proms. I'd like to turn my book *The Necessity of Poverty* into an opera, based on the idea that it might be fun to discuss the gap between rich and poor in a kind of recitative. Not *The Beggar's Opera* updated, nor a *Threepenny Opera*. Rather something more stringent and perhaps strident.

I spoke at a fund-raising event at St Martin in the Fields last Christmas and I sang the *Kyrie eleison*. They didn't ask me to – they asked me to give a talk, but I said 'before I do my talk I'd like to do what I've always wanted to do', and so I sang *Kyrie eleison* – and I got them all singing!

I'm on my third family, so even though I'm a 68-year-old guy I've got very young children and I'm always singing to them. All my kids have always said: 'Dad, where do you get all those songs from?' If we're in the car I don't like the radio on because you can't quite hear it in the back, so if we're going on a journey I'll sing. And they're all learning the songs. With my family being Irish I know lots of songs and I love folksongs – it's good for you to keep singing. **G**
To support The Big Issue, visit bigissue.org.uk

Cate Blanchett

The actor in 2022 on how music informs her life and work, especially when playing a conductor in the feature film, Tár

Often when I'm creating roles – and obviously in this one because it is so much about the aural experience – your connection to a character will be through a piece of music. It's something I can't put words to – and I'm always looking to dispense with words, particularly in films: 'Do you need to say this, or can we do this with a gesture. Maybe if I just move very quickly here, or move very slowly there, I'll reveal far more through a gesture than through language?' Not that I am a dancer, but if I had my time over I would love to dispense with language altogether and just move through space. That's the point I connected with the conducting experience – it's often through the way they breathe, the most minuscule gestures, that the orchestra understands – particularly an orchestra who has worked with a conductor many, many times.

I learnt piano as a girl, and whenever I've been pregnant I've said 'well, I'm going to finally finish my degree, and I'm going to pick up the piano again …' But of course one thing happens, and then another thing happens, and tragically it's not until I get asked to do something for a role – to play Bach in a film – that I feel I can finally indulge. I had to brush up on it. I was in Budapest at the time and there was a wonderful teacher from the Academy. She was so fantastic about the discipline of Bach, and both the freedom that is given to you within each phrase but also the mathematical precision that is absolutely vital. Part of the scene in the film – and it's a very long scene – is this desperate desire to communicate with a student, and one way that my character tries to communicate with him is to show him that even within what seems to be the rigid structure of Bach, there is this incredible freedom.

I think about *Death and the Maiden* a lot. The music of Górecki too. During the making of this film – and this was something I hadn't ever done before – I thought I wanted to have music in my head the whole time, so when people were talking to me I had an earpiece in where I would just have various pieces of music playing. And Todd [Field, *Tár*'s writer and director] kept referring to a piece of Górecki's that he called the 'Tár march' – a particular rhythm that he wanted her to walk to.

I had a really amazing experience about 10 years ago. Alex Ross gave a lecture series with the Australian Chamber Orchestra, conducted by Richard Tognetti, and when I went to that I heard Xenakis's music performed live. And you know that there are moments in one's listening – and it's usually the live experience – when everything gets shifted off its axis. And I remember in that moment thinking: 'I have never heard this before, I have never felt like this before, and I can't unhear this'.

THE RECORD I COULDN'T LIVE WITHOUT

Stravinsky The Rite of Spring
New York PO / Leonard Bernstein
Sony Classical
If I need to be shaken up and discombobulated, I put on the Rite of Spring.

I think the *Rite of Spring* is amazing – it's such a shock to the system, your blood flows differently after listening to it. And I also like anything with a cello solo, because it's so close to the human voice.

When I was in High School, I had a friend whose uncle was an opera critic, and whenever I'd go to his house, it would be silent. And I said to him 'it's interesting, your world is music and you don't have music on'. And he said 'I listen to music, it's not background. I sit, and I listen to it'. And it was quite a new concept to me because that wasn't the case in my household. Obviously if you go to a concert you attend to the music in a very different way, which is why I find it such a profound experience hearing music live. But I can no longer have music in the background. My world now falls into two zones – it falls into the times when I'm listening to music, and the times when I'm not. It's quite a different shift to me. **G**

Matthew Bourne

The choreographer and founder of New Adventures dance-theatre company talked to us in 2018 about his desire to immerse himself in every score he uses

If you're going to take a much-loved score like *Swan Lake* and do something different with it, as I have, you've got to love it. And I think it's glorious music. What's so wonderful about it for me, as a creator, is that it's written to tell a story (albeit a different one to mine!). It's dramatically driven, which is a gift to someone like me who loves telling stories. My 2018 version of *Swan Lake* has had a few revisions – it's more grown-up, more gorgeous – but audiences will still recognise it from the 1995 production. Yes, there are cuts to the score – any company will do that – but it's in a recognisable order.

I was about 18 when I saw my first ballet – and that just happened to be *Swan Lake*. I grew up in East London with parents who loved popular music and music from the movies; my dad would be downstairs singing Frank Sinatra, and I'd be upstairs singing Julie Andrews or Barbra Streisand. I had a big collection of LPs, but the only classical one was Holst's *The Planets*. So when I left school (which I'd hated) I decided to educate myself, culturally, in areas I didn't know anything about. I'd never seen an opera, so I decided I should go to one to see if I liked it. The same happened with ballet – and that's how I ended up seeing *Swan Lake*. Having grown up with MGM musicals, I now discovered that you could see a piece with dancing all the way through it. That was how I fell in love with ballet and contemporary dance.

It was interesting when, more than 20 years ago now, we approached Tchaikovsky's score afresh. I'd often felt that, in the classical version of the ballet, Act 4 struggled to express the emotional turmoil of the music so it was nice to be able to address that. We were also able to think about what the tempi should be. The classical version had become progressively slower as dancers challenged themselves with higher jumps, more turns, greater extensions ... So we decided to look at the movement of actual swans and use that to inspire the tempi. It was lovely to be more faithful to the original score.

One score that really rewards you through repeated listening is Prokofiev's *Cinderella*, which I choreographed back in 1997. The Prokofiev estate loved what we did with it, and they've now trusted us to create a reduced score of *Romeo and Juliet* for our new production that opens next year. The music will be arranged for 15 musicians by our regular New Adventures collaborator Terry Davies; the aim is to produce something that's true to Prokofiev but that's exciting and refreshing – a different sound for what will be a contemporary reimagining of Shakespeare's classic love story.

Live music is a dilemma for us. We're not a ballet company that gets funded to the level where we can tour with a full orchestra. But live music is something we strive for, and in *Swan Lake*, for the London run at Sadler's Wells, we're

THE RECORD I COULDN'T LIVE WITHOUT

Rodgers & Hammerstein Climb Ev'ry Mountain (from The Sound of Music OST) Sony
Something about this hits me every time – the introduction, the chords ... I adore it, and I've already told my partner that I want it played at my funeral.

bringing in top musicians to perform a reduced score. We also have, in London, the Royal Ballet's Matthew Ball dancing with us. It's a dream role for him – it was after he saw the show at the age of eight that he decided he wanted to be a dancer.

With any new project, I do a lot of research. For *The Red Shoes* [2016], I'd wanted to do my own version for a long time, but there wasn't enough music in the film. I also found the original score by Brian Easdale very much 'of its time'. So I listened to the music by Bernard Herrmann, focusing on the non-Hitchcock film scores he wrote around the time of *The Red Shoes* such as *The Ghost and Mrs Muir* and *Fahrenheit 451*, and then Terry brought it all together.

When I'm working on a piece, I'll listen to the music on my iPod or play it through my Sonus system. I have Spotify, which is useful when you're in the studio and need to listen to something instantly. I still like to 'own' music though – it's only when I buy music on CD that I feel like it's mine. **G**
Visit new-adventures.net for details of Matthew Bourne's productions

Frank Gehry

The architect, talking to Gramophone in 2010, on how to create intimacy between orchestras and audiences when designing a hall

My mother used to take me to concerts in Toronto to hear Sir Ernest MacMillan. During the week I would often see Sir Ernest biking through the park – and he'd wave to me, though he didn't know who I was. So that was the beginning. Mahler, Tchaikovsky, Beethoven, Bach – I've found inspiration in the structures of their pieces, and the aural spaces that they create.

By some good fortune I was asked to work at the Hollywood Bowl by Ernest Fleischmann; we became good friends and he became my de facto music teacher. Through him I met every major conductor and soloist who came through town. I enjoyed meeting Pierre Boulez – I first experienced him at the rug concerts in New York, where I sat on stage on the carpet and faced the conductors. He doesn't wave his arms and so if you're in the audience behind him you don't see what he's doing, but facing him was the first time I'd experienced that the expression of passion can come from the simplest of things, so I've always revered him.

So I got to know him, and composers like John Adams, Steven Stucky, and Esa-Pekka Salonen – I actually collaborated with him on *Wing on Wing*, a work for the opening of the Walt Disney Hall. It was embarrassing because he asked me to talk, recorded me, and told me he would garble it so that my voice would be unrecognisable. I got to the concert, and I'm sitting in the fancy seats, and all of a sudden out of the blue, I hear myself say 'why the fish!' Later, he told me he changed it so that it's not so obvious. Esa-Pekka was here for so long, and I got to know him so well. I grew up in Canada, and the climate in Finland is very similar – there's a kind of Canadian shyness that the Finns have too, so I could relate to him in that way.

The thing that helped me in designing Disney Hall was the access to all these people. We built models, and Boulez spent a day inside my model – I remember passing him a sandwich. The thing you learn about musicians – or I have over the years – is they can sense aural space, can adjust to it. He just sat there, and said, 'It's going to work'.

You know what happens when an orchestra plays in a hall for a long time? Over time the physical tightness disintegrates. So what I was looking at in the Dorothy Chandler Pavilion when I started this was a sloppy mess, and I mentioned this to Esa-Pekka. Because of that we took the orchestra to Royce Hall and reorganised it. We made a much tighter relationship between the players, and we measured that; we built the risers and put them in the Chandler. It was a very detailed assessment of every part of the relationship of the orchestra.

If the performers can hear each other – and the hall has to allow them to hear each other – they play better; when they play

THE RECORD I COULDN'T LIVE WITHOUT

Mendelssohn Piano Trios
Emanuel Ax *pf* **Yo-Yo Ma** *vc* **Itzhak Perlman** *vn*
Sony Classics
This recording is very beautiful. I have it on my iPod - it was a gift from Manny.

better the audience feels it and responds; and the orchestra senses that, so it's a geometric progression of approval going both ways. You can see it, it's palpable, and the audience talks about it. They're sitting 100ft away, but how close they feel to the players – and the musicians tell me how intimate the performance feels – that's a magic trick, and it's really imperative to understand that when designing a concert hall.

So all of that experience has gone into the New World Symphony's hall in Miami. It's a smaller hall, so it's not as hard to create this intimacy. Miami is an experimental place – it's a teaching laboratory. The experience of Michael Tilson Thomas teaching on a small TV is powerful, but imagine that blown up to an image that's bigger than life. And he'll be on stage with his orchestra communicating with a youth orchestra in another country.

It's my favourite thing to do, building for music and art. It's more intuitive if you're working with people who work in the same way that you do, and think like you do. The collaboration between two people who are in sync can take you to heights. It's about being open – I think if we knew where we were going we wouldn't do it. It's all work in progress. **G**

Richard E Grant

The actor in 2010 on how classical music has provided the perfect context for his life and work

My parents had a big classical music record collection. By the age of 10 I knew *Aida* in particular extremely well – they played that over and over. We had the Karajan recording with Carlo Bergonzi and Renata Tebaldi, which is still my favourite. For various reasons that opera and recording resonated very deeply with me. I suppose because it was set in Africa, even though it is thousands of miles north of where I lived in Swaziland, it gave me a natural connection.

It was in 1969, when I was 12 years old, that my father decided that we should travel to Europe for some cultural injection. He took us on a trip around European cities and then to England, and we went to see a show or movie every day for six weeks. In Rome we saw *Aida* with Gwyneth Jones. We'd been in the city for a week and the only seats my father could get were in a box practically on the stage. It was a traditional, enormous, spectacular production – seeing elephants on stage a few feet away, at the age of 12, has a big effect! It was a seminal occasion for me, one of my first major theatrical experiences. It afforded me a glimpse into the sheer power of theatre.

There was an emotional side to it as well. My parents had just got divorced and my father had remarried, so the resonance of this Verdian love triangle didn't escape me. It seemed to me then almost as a larger-scale version of my parents' lives, although they didn't end up in a tomb singing to each other.

I had an inspired Scottish piano teacher, Bunny Barnes, who was responsible for my musical education. I became obsessed with all sorts of different composers, Mahler in particular. Bunny said, 'Mahler is an adolescent phase you will go through and mature beyond'. He still remains a great favourite, though, so clearly that maturation hasn't occurred!

It was incredibly lucky for me, in a small town of 15,000 people, albeit a capital, to have someone so passionate about music to educate me beyond what I could play on the piano and get me listening to things outside what I would normally encounter. She thought that Mozart and Beethoven were the great masters of everything. She tried to convince me that Tchaikovsky was kitsch and that the Second Piano Concerto of Shostakovich was also questionable, so I found myself having to fight these prejudices. Yet she spoke to me as though I were an adult, with no patronising, and when you're that age that is unusual and invigorating.

The first night I arrived in England to live was April 24, 1982, just as boats were leaving Portsmouth to fight in the Falklands. I headed to the Royal Festival Hall to hear Pogorelich play Chopin's Second Piano Concerto. That was my first adventure in a journey into London's musical life – a musical life of incredible dimensions – that I never tire of.

THE RECORD I COULDN'T LIVE WITHOUT

Mozart Flute Concertos
Sharon Bezaly fl / Ostrobothnian CO / Juha Kangas
BIS
Mozart's flute concertos seem to me to be the most pure and beautiful music I've ever heard.

Almost all my work is informed by music. I became a professional actor at around the time that the Walkman appeared, so being able to have music playing in your head, privately, became very useful and I've used that for atmosphere, for the mood, for research on every job I've ever done.

Francis Ford Coppola used music like that when filming *Dracula*. He'd play music on set to create the atmosphere he wanted for the screen. As an actor that was very helpful and I used the same tactic to direct my own autobiographical film *Wah-Wah* six years ago. Standing on a mountainside to recreate my father's bizarre funeral, I put an iPod into a set of speakers and played a piece by Cape Town-born composer Abdullah Ibrahim. It's the most wonderfully melancholic, nostalgic-sounding music and everyone – 120-plus people consisting of crew, actors and extras – instantly picked up the right mood. It was the first time on the set that the first assistant director didn't have to shout for quiet before we shot. **G**

Baroness Susan Greenfield

Scientist Baroness Susan Greenfield reflected in 2010 on the relationship between classical music and the way our brains work

Music was never really in my family. I've got quite a philistine background in that sense. Any love of music that I have came from school. The first time I'm conscious of music making an impression on me is at primary school, where they played Britten's *The Young Person's Guide to the Orchestra* as we filed into assembly. They taught us about the orchestra there, and I learnt to play the recorder. I was rather better at the triangle, though!

When I went to my secondary school my parents wanted me to learn an instrument and decided that it would be lovely for me to play the violin. Well, it wasn't lovely in my hands! So that was a short-lived affair. Also, I'm not quite tone-deaf but I'm far from a great singer – virtually all my friends were in the choir but I wasn't. I loved and still love singing and hear it all the time in my head, yet when I open my mouth something else comes out.

Because I didn't have a background or formal education in music, my experiences of it have been piecemeal. One of the first pieces that greatly moved me was Carl Orff's *Carmina Burana*. I saw it when I was at university, performed at Oxford Town Hall. It was the sheer drama of the thing that appealed to me. And it was drama again that struck me when I first heard Beethoven's Ninth Symphony with its busy, large-scale fourth movement. And again when I heard Gershwin's *Rhapsody in Blue* – the way it starts whimsically, with a reedy noise that eventually builds to a fantastically exciting climax.

This starts to move thought on music to the idea of continuity. Reflecting on the continuity of theme, on the way the structure is built in the Gershwin, for instance, leads one to think about music's mental function. This kind of continuity is something I feel strongly is missing in the prevalent current cultures.

I deeply feel that there is a natural order to things. Much classical music internalises a sequence of things, a beginning, a middle and an end. Pop music, raves, techno, all of these things are about a sensory experience in the moment rather than a long sequence or continuity.

This is reflected in ideas of the difference between thought and mere moments of consciousness. One difference is that when you have a thought there is always something it leads to – a memory, a train of logic, a fantasy – whereas when you're just feeling something there isn't a sequence. That's all mirrored in the way you read and write. So that sense of sequence, of beginning, middle and end, and indeed past, present and future, is very deep in the human brain.

It is part of growing up. Small children need to rehearse this sense of sequence. The brain needs to work to become good at it. That's why you have stories read to you, because you're

THE RECORD I COULDN'T LIVE WITHOUT

Mozart Così fan tutte
Soloists; Concerto Köln / René Jacobs
Harmonia Mundi
The way the music undulates so beautifully in the lovers' tender duets is so moving.

training your brain to have, again, that sense of beginning, middle and end. Just as you do when you frame a sentence.

I worry that people who spend a lot of time not dealing with words or music in sequences aren't training their brain enough to structure their thinking in a deep sense. They then become like small children, or somewhat even like Alzheimer's patients. They become disorientated and confused because they can't measure the present up against their previous experience and conceptual framework. And if they don't have a sense of sequence then actions don't seem to have consequences in the same way – and if they don't have consequences then they don't seem to have meaning. Things only have meaning when they have an idea of permanence. And if a person's actions don't have meaning, there can be an implication then that the person doesn't have meaning either.

One place where you can certainly see how music has been used is religion. The social anthropologist Harvey Whitehouse has talked about religiosity and the ways of imprinting on the brain, and one is through rhythmic repetition. Now think of Gregorian chant. Classical music is so powerful and in many ways so important. Ⓖ

Sir Nicholas Grimshaw

The architect in 2005 on hearing Handel at
Glyndebourne and building his first concert hall

Music has always been a way of getting out of myself.
People talk about being transported by music, and it
certainly does this for me. It is an alternative to my
fairly frenetic existence in the architectural world.

I think the live aspect of music is very important. I particularly
like going to live performances; I see it almost in the same way
as going to the theatre. As a student I used to go the Proms and
walk around the gallery of the Albert Hall. It was never good
acoustically. It mashed up music like a food mixer. I did use to
play LPs when I was drawing, but I've never been quite so much
into CDs, especially early ones which I found too clinical.

I went to the Aldeburgh Festival this year where Thomas
Adès conducted the Northern Sinfonia in Beethoven's Fourth
Symphony. He played it as though it had been written last
week – a most extraordinarily interesting rendering of it. There
was absolute precision there: it sounded like every phrase had
been thought about and turned round in his head.

I can remember seeing Adès playing the piano in somebody's
house when he was a kid – there is music in his bones. He's
genuinely experimental and enormously dedicated; I don't
think he'd do anything unless he could put the necessary time
and effort into it, and that is the exact reverse of the nightmare
thing many other conductors have to do – often performing 200
concerts a year, 'It's Friday so it must be Helsinki' and so on.

Music is a search for quality, exactly the same as in architecture –
you try to build to the highest quality, precision and beauty
that you can. You can have routine concerts where symphonies
are churned out just like office buildings are churned out. And
I don't think that does much for anybody. But a performance
where you've got a really dedicated orchestra and conductor
raises the music to a completely different level.

I recently went to Glyndebourne to hear Handel's *Julius Caesar*
conducted by William Christie. There was some fun in it, some
levity, some dancing to the music – it's got a wonderful sort of
bouncy rhythm – and I thought that Handel would have liked
that. The very, very slow build on that piece is fascinating – it's
four hours, give or take – and the drama gradually builds very,
very carefully with the music. Christie is another conductor
who is totally in control of the orchestra and understands early
instruments and what you can get out of them. We used to go
to the Tours music festival in France a lot, which took place in
a 13th-century barn – a wonderful building! I used to sit there
with my head up looking at the structure all the way through.
I remember one year hearing Richter and Radu Lupu play four-
handed jazz at the party afterwards. I asked Radu Lupu 'How
did it feel?', because after the performance he'd been fêted and
they'd been throwing flowers on stage. He said 'Oh, I don't
think I played very well tonight'. He was quite genuine, he

THE RECORD I COULDN'T LIVE WITHOUT

Adès These Premises are Alarmed
CBSO / Thomas Adès Warner Classics
I thought this was a terrifically witty piece - I'm
a terrific fan of Adès. It also has an architectural
angle to it I suppose!

wasn't being pretentious, he was just assessing himself, and the
public was neither here nor there really.

Keeping people going to live performances is something I'm
very keen on, which is one of the reasons I'm now patron of
a little music festival in Norfolk which was launched in July
this year – the North Norfolk Music Festival in South Creake.
It is held in a wonderful church that seats about 400. The
artistic directors Simon Rowland-Jones and Barry Cheesman
put together an absolutely fascinating programme – artists
included Dame Josephine Barstow, baritone Stephan Loges
and the Doric Quartet. (The vicar is very keen on music, so
that helps.) We had the most abominable weather – torrential
rain – and I thought that for people to turn out on an evening
like that and tramp through a churchyard with umbrellas
showed that the need to hear music is there to be tapped. I've
vowed to write an article for next year's festival programme
about the history of string music in churches.

My architectural practice is building a concert hall in
Troy, near Albany in upstate New York, for the Rensselaer
Polytechnic Institute. Hopefully it should open sometime
next year, and for an architect that's quite a big day – the first
concert in your first concert hall. I shall certainly be there! **G**

Sir Anthony Hopkins

Acting may have made his name, but it wasn't his first choice of career, as he told us in 2009

Music was my first desire, my first wish – and then I became an actor. I started playing the piano aged six, but wasn't very adept at it. I never had the situation to practise very much and so it was a pretty indecisive introduction to music. But I soon realised that I wanted to be involved and started composing at an early age, writing for the piano.

I wrote a piece in 1957 when I was 20. I didn't know what a score looked like, so I went to the library and found a score of *Sheherazade*. I figured out how to put a score together and started putting this piece of mine down on paper, and it was kind of evocative. It was all improvised; the thing lasted about 10 minutes. Eventually, though, I abandoned the ambition. I wanted to be a musician more, but acting is how I made my living.

Many years later, in 1994, I made a film called *August*, which I wrote and directed as well as acted in. The producer knew that I sometimes wrote music and suggested I compose the score. I wanted George Fenton to do it, but he was busy. 'I hear you play the piano,' he said at our meeting, and asked me to demonstrate. I was so in awe of musicians I didn't want to play, but he insisted, and I played him something I'd written and he thought it beautiful and said I must write my own score. So I used that same piece from 40 years earlier in the soundtrack. Suddenly I was a composer writing for a film and most recently the Dallas Symphony Orchestra has put on a concert of some of my music. The audience jumped up and down at the end and called for me to conduct, which I did. And that was fun. It was strange.

I don't take any of it seriously though. I paint as well but I'm very laid back about it all – about acting too, now.

It's a bit of a paradox. All of these creative things – acting, composing and painting – I do work hard at them all and care about them, but at the same time it's all just for sheer enjoyment. It's like with acting. I learn the text thoroughly and of course that's difficult, and as I'm learning the part I think about it and interpretations come to me. Currently, I'm learning King Lear for a planned film, and ideas are running through my head. But then I have to let go. In music too, if I'm too painstaking, it'll be a mess.

I'm writing a piece for piano and orchestra over the next two weeks and I don't know where I'm going with it. I do care about it. I do have a passion. But not so I want to tear my hair out! Judi Dench and Michael Gambon, great actors, don't agonise over their art. They take it seriously but don't wallow. I love America and American artists, but so many are so miserable. You don't have to suffer to be creative.

THE RECORD I COULDN'T LIVE WITHOUT

Schumann The Merry Peasant
Rico Gulda *pf* Naxos
I was tortured by that piece when I was a little kid. I had to play it as a piano exercise again and again. But how I love Schumann!

You also don't have to spell everything out. I try to keep my music suggestive. It's like when I played Hannibal Lecter in *The Silence of the Lambs*. I portrayed him as civilised and quite charming. Audiences were terrified – because I knew they would fill in the gaps and realise he's a fiend. Similarly, I wrote a piece of music called *Slipstream*, where I had a high-pitched cello and then the violin slid in underneath it and then I touched in things, like a guitar coming in contrapuntally. You suggest and listeners do the rest.

I suppose I'm drawn to music with some sort of complexity. You carry things with you from your childhood. I know that I bring a psychological complexity to roles and although I am very cheerful in life, there is a melancholy side to me that I've carried from my youth in Wales. I love the sounds of Vaughan Williams and Elgar; I love their melancholy as well as their pastoral qualities.

Music often helps me find a way into roles. I listened to Copland all the time when preparing to play Richard Nixon on film. But above all, I adore listening to music across many styles. I have an instinctive appreciation. I'm free of the burden of analysis, free of the bondage of worrying about how it works; I don't have that kind of brain. I just love it. **G**

Barry Humphries

In 2016 the late comedian and actor told us about his journey from discovering classical music in Melbourne to creating a show celebrating the music of the Weimar Republic

When I was a schoolboy in Melbourne we had quite a good library and I stumbled upon Constant Lambert's famous book, *Music Ho!*, published in 1934, the year I was born. I was fascinated to read about all these composers I'd never heard of, and Lambert's very idiosyncratic appraisals, or dismissals, and I thought I needed to hear this music. We'd started at the school what was called a gramophone society – incidentally I still call my CD player a gramophone – and we used, at lunchtime on Tuesdays, to play records. The society met in the physics laboratory where there was a turntable and decent speaker. I remember particularly listening to Copland's *El Salón México*, which I don't like much now, but I remember the orchestral colouring appealed to me. And then there was Respighi, a composer who I still like, something like the *Fountains of Rome*. But I was very interested in the composers that Lambert referred to. He admired Darius Milhaud for example, and Kurt Weill. He wrote about the influence of jazz on classical music, which of course infected his own work, particularly the *Rio Grande* and the Piano Concerto.

I would write off to a shop in Monmouth Street, London, called Collectors Corner. I requested *The Threepenny Opera*, of which there was an HMV recording of highlights made about 1931, Milhaud's *La Création du monde* and *L'Histoire du soldat* by Stravinsky. And back they came, many months later, beautiful packed in mini wooden crates, and I played them lovingly with fibre needles. Some friends and I used to listen to music at home and we had little, rather pretentious, soirées. You can imagine these schoolboys in a suburb of Melbourne in 1950 listening to this extraordinary music. We would listen to the Beecham recordings of Delius – there would be the sounds of Delius wafting out on the Melbourne night air.

Before I went into the theatre I had a job which lasted a whole year in the Melbourne offices of EMI. It was at the time of the transition from 78s to LPs, and for copyright reasons all 78s had to be broken. Don't ask me why. So my job was to break records with a hammer every day. It was terrible. Whole sets of Arnold Bax, I remember that. It was a totally Dadaist task.

Going to concerts was a social habit in Europe, but in the colonies, you know, not so. But we did have the advantage – a tragic one really – of hosting so many refugees, and many of them were musicians, and they really did bring to that funny, philistine world of Australia in that decade of the 1940s and late 1930s something that we would never have had otherwise. They became teachers, and composers and performers.

THE RECORD I COULDN'T LIVE WITHOUT

Weill The Threepenny Opera
Historic original recordings 1928-44
Capriccio
This strange music, which isn't music hall, vaudeville or operetta, captivated me. And I still love it.

In a second-hand bookshop I came across a pile of sheet music which had been brought to Australia by one of the many German and Austrian Jewish refugees. It was totally unfamiliar music, except there was the name again of Kurt Weill, which I remembered from Lambert and my own record. So I bought up all this music for practically nothing. Then recently, when I had an association with the Australian Chamber Orchestra, I suggested an evening of this submerged, overlooked repertoire. To call our show Weimar Cabaret is really incorrect. There are cabaret elements which a cabaret performer, a wonderful girl called Meow Meow, sings, and couple of these things we do together. But there's also a lot of orchestral music – we open for example with Hindemith, not a composer Constant Lambert liked very much. And then we've got a lot of very unfamiliar music, often very jazzy. It's music just before the cataclysm, it's music just before Hitler, before really Western civilization came to an end. And so it has a great poignancy as well as humour and beauty. **ⓖ**

Armando Iannucci

The writer and director talked to us in 2006
about the joy of making musical discoveries

My interest in classical music began in my first year at secondary school, when the teacher played *The Planets* in the music appreciation class. At the time I shared a bedroom with an older brother who was into Pink Floyd and Deep Purple, and I always remember thinking 'I just don't get this. Am I just odd?' So when I heard classical music at school I thought 'that's it, that's what I like!'

Fortunately at roughly the same time Glasgow City Council built a new municipal library with a fantastic classical music section, and I was allowed to take out two or three vinyls on my ticket. I tended to gravitate towards big, lush orchestral pieces like Mahler, Bruckner, Wagner and Strauss. Using that, and the radio, I set about finding out as much as I could.

At that time – and more or less to this day – I couldn't read music, so technically I was completely musically illiterate. But in the last year or so I've taken up the piano (my wife bought me one for my 40th birthday) and go to weekly lessons with a lady in the next village. I'm starting absolutely from scratch – it's going slowly, but we're edging towards Grade 1. I just want to be able to play some slow pieces of Bach, like the aria from the *Goldberg Variations*, or some of the slower preludes or fugues – that will do for me, I've no plans to go any further.

When I'm writing I always have music on, right through the day. I tend to think musically when I'm editing and filming. I recently did a Channel 4 series, and sometimes when I'd come up with a story I knew the pieces of music that would go alongside it, and would shoot it with them in mind – I found myself going back to the standards like Pärt, Shostakovich and Vaughan Williams.

I love Ligeti and find him fascinating. When I was 13 or 14 I was quite into avant-garde pieces, and would listen to BBC Radio 3's late-night concerts of strange electronic music, Xenakis and Ligeti. I had no conception of atonality or serialism, no idea of what the musical theory was behind it, but the noises were quite interesting, quite dramatic. They sort of told a story.

Haydn I think is fantastic, whereas Mozart just does nothing for me. I don't dislike him, but for some reason I feel totally detached from his music. I don't know what it is: too polished, too perfectly formed? I like the *Jupiter* Symphony and the Overture to *The Marriage of Figaro* – and that's it. When I mention it to people I do get the odd one who says 'yes, I know what you mean'. I think there's a club of us out there!

I'm always listening to new sounds and composers I haven't come across before. There's a great guy I discovered recently called Weinberg, a contemporary of Shostakovich. It does make you think how an accident of fate – that he happened to be around at the same time as Shostakovich and that Shostakovich was probably a bit better – means that Shostakovich is

THE RECORD I COULDN'T LIVE WITHOUT

Haydn Last Piano Sonatas
Glenn Gould *pf*
Sony Classical
The opening of HobXVI/48 – it just sounds mad, like some late-night jazz.

remembered and Weinberg forgotten. There are also lot of English symphonies written in the '60s and '70s that I like exploring – Rubbra, Simpson and people like that.

I find people talk less to each other about music than they do about literature. I think there's something about music, that the generalist feels that unless you have the intellectual background, you're not equipped to talk about it. And that's a great shame. Even when you go to a concert, as you're leaving all you hear is people saying: 'well, shall we get a taxi now?' But a concert is a very dramatic event – the physical presence of all these people.

I certainly think there is less of a barrier to classical music today. There is, for want of a better word, a coolness to it that unfortunately leads to a certain amount of 'packaging' – but actually that's not such a bad thing, in that it doesn't put people off and it doesn't make them embarrassed to have it on their iPod. It was interesting how many people downloaded the nine symphonies during Radio 3's Beethoven week, so there is a hunger there. People want to be led to stuff that has a bit of meat to it, that you have to work at, and isn't just all the nice bits of Chopin on one CD. People are now asking: where did this come from? What else is there? **G**

Eric Idle

The former Python told us in 2007 about his Sullivan obsession ... and an updated Messiah

For my generation, music first touched many of us in the forms of Elvis, the Everly Brothers and their like. When that late-1950s wave went away, I discovered classical music and jazz. Then The Beatles came along and it was OK to like pop music again. But the love of classical stayed with me, and I listen to 90 per cent classical music all day and have done most of my life.

At school in Wolverhampton they had a good collection of recordings, which was a lifeline – boarding school being a brutal place for me. The only thing about an unhappy childhood is that it can give you so much better a life. I learnt to retreat into my head and music became an escape, a way to fill all those hours. I can cope with almost everything now, including, I should think, prison.

Early loves included Brahms and of course Gilbert and Sullivan. Many years later, playing Ko-Ko in *The Mikado* at English National Opera changed my life. The director Jonathan Miller gave me my second career when he asked me to update the lyrics of Ko-Ko's patter song. At a stroke I became a musical comedy writer.

I love that form. Immediately I finished *The Mikado* I knew I wanted to write a musical. Musical comedy had died; it had become all about helicopters and big effects – MTV theatre. There was a cultural void waiting to be filled.

One idea I had in the 1980s was to turn Mel Brooks' film *The Producers* into a musical. I would have played Bloom, Mel himself Bialystock and Jonathan Miller would have directed. But Mel finally declined; he was devoted to making movies at the time. It was when I went to see his stage version of *The Producers* years later I knew I could sell *Spamalot*. The audience just went 'yes!' – they realised that they'd been missing this vital thing called laughter.

Sullivan remained my inspiration. *Spamalot* is very much a musical written by a Ko-Ko. Sullivan himself was always funny; his *Ivanhoe* period only came late on when Queen Victoria wanted him to get serious. In that first flush of his talent, when he first partnered Gilbert, he had that wonderful sense of a lightness of touch. He had great tunes in his head, and as a lover of Schubert also had a natural sense of how melody should work.

Cleverly, Sullivan doesn't give a nudge and a wink the entire time. It's a constant balance between light and darkness – and that's very Dickens, a very Victorian strain. I find in my shows that you can get very close to real emotion and still be moving. It isn't just parody. When one character sings about being alone in *Spamalot*, people have actually cried, but yet they can see it's funny.

THE RECORD I COULDN'T LIVE WITHOUT

Handel Messiah
Freiburger Barockorchester / René Jacobs
Harmonia Mundi
It has to be Handel's *Messiah* – I just have to hear it every week.

Similarly, 'Always look on the bright side of life' is a war song at heart. The Monty Python team inherited that genre, it's what we came in with – 'The White Cliffs of Dover'. We just put inverted commas around it, and lo and behold, it becomes funny! Now, ironically, ours has actually become a wartime song; it was sung in the Falklands on HMS Sheffield, and then in the Gulf War.

There's so much that tickles you and very little in the world that actually moves you. That's what is so reassuring about classical music; it doesn't have to be funny. It gets to places that are deeper. At a time when everything is aiming for superficiality, classical music shows the bravery of not compromising. Art is finally about putting your feelings on the line.

That said, each musical form lasts about 80 years. Jazz does that, rock'n'roll does that and the symphonic form does that. After that time, you reach the limits of what you can explore and of course the freshness and freedom of being first into a field is gone. We Pythons were first in a field with TV comedy so we could go anywhere we liked. It was much harder for those who came afterwards.

I'm about to combine comedy and music again with a Handel-style oratorio based on The Life of Brian, entitled *Not The Messiah (He's A Very Naughty Boy)*. We're doing it, conducted by my cousin Peter Oundjian, at the Caramoor and Toronto festivals. It jumps into different classical genres and whole realms of fun, with numbers like 'Hail to the shoe'. The idea is to attract a different crowd back into the concert hall. **G**

Alex Jennings

The actor in 2012 on his love for Britten's music and on finding inspiration by working with such opera stars as Bryn Terfel

The music in my house when I was growing up included fairly mainstream popular classical played on gramophone records by my mum – Verdi, Puccini and so on. From my father it was jazz, so there was always a mixture in the house. That's absolutely the springboard – my tastes came from that.

I can't really remember exactly when I discovered Benjamin Britten, as that certainly wasn't through my mum. It was when I was at university – the end of the '70s – that I started going with friends to concerts, and I remember seeing *Peter Grimes* at the Opera House with Jon Vickers, which was a pretty gobsmacking event. I was absolutely bowled over by it and by him – not just his singing but his acting abilities. And I know I saw the *War Requiem* around this time. I kind of discovered a love for Britten myself, really.

Having read a lot about him and having played him in *The Habit of Art*, I hear his sort of struggles in his music – and the Englishness of it, I suppose – and I've always had connections with that part of the world. Psychologically, his work is so captivating and exciting. I find just listening to *The Turn of the Screw* really disturbing – terrifying really! After I finished *The Habit of Art* I got to go to the Red House in Aldeburgh, the house Britten shared with Peter Pears, and stayed there, sleeping in one of the bedrooms, which was slightly weird. It's an incredible house: you absolutely feel their presence there still.

For me, opera, when the acting convinces, is sensational. Again, it's mostly Britten that's really moved me in the opera house – there was that brilliant production of *Peter Grimes* that was at the Coliseum a couple of years ago. And Nick Hytner's opera productions – I've worked with him a lot and seen his work in the opera house, his *Julius Caesar* in Paris, his *Xerxes* – have been particular highlights in my opera-going life.

I've been really fortunate over the last few years to work alongside some opera singers. I did a production of *Candide* at the Coliseum and *My Fair Lady* at the Châtelet in Paris the Christmas before last – and I'm going to be doing that again next year. I did a gala at the Opera House recently with Bryn Terfel, and to be in a pretty small room next to him – it's been an amazing experience to see him work, a huge privilege to be up close to that power and that awesome acting talent as well.

It's been fantastic to work alongside singers who are coming at it, generally, from a completely different direction to me. It was amazing to work with Toby Spence in *Candide*. They approach it very differently to how we work in theatre – it's terrifying as well, the first time we did the sing-through of *Candide* they all came knowing it, which is not what we do. Working with an

THE RECORD I COULDN'T LIVE WITHOUT

Britten War Requiem
Soloists; LSO / Benjamin Britten
Decca
This is such a rich work, and the rehearsal extract, with Britten coaxing the performers, is a real bonus.

orchestra is brilliant and the impression I've got is – because I'm not a great singer at all, but I act my way through the songs – that they quite enjoyed it (or they told me they did) because, working with someone who's not quite so rigidly stuck to the notes, no two nights are ever quite the same!

I'm looking forward to performing in Alan Bennett's *Hymn*. George Fenton had a commission 10 or 11 years ago to write a piece for the Medici String Quartet and he got Alan on board. It's a mixture of music and narration, and it's about the formative musical influences in Alan's earlier life, of listening to the Hallé and English popular music of the time, palm court orchestra music, and Elgar and Vaughan Williams. The narration weaves in and out with the music; sometimes it's concurrent with the music and sometimes the music takes over. It's a fantastic piece. Alan did some performances 10 years ago but doesn't want to do it any more, so he handed it over to me. I'll also be doing a new short play that Alan has written about himself and his parents. So I've become sort of Alan Bennett-by-proxy, which is slightly weird but very nice! And George's music for this piece is wonderful, really evocative and very moving.

I also do quite a few programmes with Lucy Parham of Debussy's piano music and writings, and another one about George Sand and Chopin. I've also done one with Andrew Kennedy and Julius Drake about Auden's poetry and Britten's songs. It's wonderful to work with people from different disciplines. **ⓖ**

HRH The Duke of Kent

The arts patron spoke to us in 2007 about his abiding love of opera and song

The art master at school was a music enthusiast and used to play us records and I think that probably first started my interest. But for years I was really much more fascinated by jazz. When I was in the Army and doing my training at Sandhurst there was one particular friend who introduced me to traditional jazz. That I still enjoy. But classical music has really taken over.

I had an extraordinary experience at about 18 when friends took me to Bayreuth. I'd not heard a note of Wagner, I knew absolutely nothing about him. But it was quite an awakening. We saw the *Ring* and a couple of other operas and to be thrown into that, completely cold with no preparation, was quite mad. Wagner has been an enthusiasm of mine ever since. The conductor was Keilberth and I've been very interested to see that those productions have just been issued.

I remember hearing a friend or member of our family playing Chopin on the piano and it is something I've loved ever since. Then gradually, like so many people, you hear more and your horizons broaden. It's a gradual process, it wasn't sudden.

My link with the London Philharmonic Orchestra came about through friendship with Georg Solti, who invited me to become Patron – getting on for 30 years ago. That's something I've treasured and hugely enjoyed over the years. I'm also Patron of Trinity College of Music – now called Trinity Laban, now that they have the dance school as well. I was there a couple of weeks ago to see the new dance studios, a remarkable building in Deptford, on the banks of the Thames. And I recently became Patron of Opera North, which I also enjoy very much, as well as of the Royal Choral Society and the period-instrument orchestra the Hanover Band. These are, in a sense, official things, but they are also the source of great pleasure. I was involved in European Music Year in 1985, which marked the anniversary of the birth of both Bach and Handel, and which involved lots of concerts all over the country. I chaired the committee in the UK. One thing that has remained from that year is the European Union Baroque Orchestra, giving young musicians around Europe the chance to gain experience of playing in an orchestra. Several hundred players must have gone through it now in 20-odd years.

I love opera. I've always been very fond of Glyndebourne; the standards are amazingly high and I love that little opera house – the sound is quite something. I go to a reasonable amount at Covent Garden and occasionally to ENO, though not enough. And, of course, to Opera North when I can.

I suppose my tastes are fairly conventional. I love much of Verdi and Puccini; I came quite late to Mozart, though I'm now passionate about his operas. A more recent discovery has been Janáček, particularly the operas which were done at

THE RECORD I COULDN'T LIVE WITHOUT

Schubert Die schöne Müllerin
Dietrich Fischer-Dieskau *bar* Gerald Moore *pf*
Warner Classics
Dietrich Fischer-Dieskau is an amazing singer and has done so much for the whole art of singing.

Glyndebourne, which were really superb – *Jenůfa* and *Kát'a Kabanová*, then later *Makropulos*.

Another great love is song, something I didn't know anything about until 20 years ago when one or two broadcasts awakened an interest in it. Now I listen a lot, particularly to Schubert and Schumann. It's a particularly intimate form of musical communication and in the hands of composers like those it's so sensitive. It expresses so much, especially the settings of great poetry – the way those composers were able to put that poetry into musical terms is quite extraordinary. The series of all the Schubert songs by Graham Johnson was a great thing and I'm glad to say I have the whole lot. It's tremendous. I had the great pleasure of presenting Graham Johnson with a Royal Philharmonic Society Award and was able to give it with great enthusiasm. Amazing as well are his notes, the books that came with the records.

I do not – sadly – play an instrument. Like so many, I had piano lessons but rather abandoned it at school. I now regret that terribly. I used to like following the score when listening to music, particularly with piano music. I have quite a lot of recordings and I listen a great deal to Radio 3, which is excellent. I was recently given an iPod – a most wonderful device! I've never downloaded anything but I take things off my own CDs, just for the ease of carrying the music around and listening to it. **G**

Myleene Klass

The Classic FM presenter on her musical childhood – and championing the artform today

I'm from six generations of classical musicians on my father's side: I was handed my grandfather's violin and was told 'this is what you're going to play'. The wonderful thing with being raised in a household where classical music was so appreciated is it's just omnipresent. I'd come down for breakfast and there would be Wagner playing, or Tchaikovsky, or Lehár – it was just a real mix, and I think that's what's so important, that exposure.

So I learned the violin – I don't remember starting it, it was just always there, I learned the piano the same way. And then at about 11 I started on the harp. It was just those flourishes, and the chords and scales that you can create that you can't create on any other instruments, the way the pedals can be operated in such a way that you could have consecutive notes next to each other that you could never, ever on any instrument replicate, that I just found fascinating.

But it was both brilliant and frustrating. The harp helped me with my teaching later down the line because my left hand could do everything it needed to do, my brain was already operating at grades 7-8, but my right hand didn't have the capability yet – and understanding that sort of frustration is very helpful if you do start teaching. I became a music teacher at the weekends when I was about 12 to get pocket money. Music was a brilliant avenue for me because it gave me financial independence – every time I won a competition or a festival I realised you could make a living from being a musician. And when I got my place at Junior Guildhall it really was the beginning of something great.

When I went to Junior Guildhall I was told I was a little bit too young to start singing – I'm a teenager at this point, and if someone says you can't do something then of course I thought 'well, then I want to sing opera!' And although my Dad speaks fluent German, and my Mum speaks Tagalog and Spanish, I hadn't really paid much attention to language, and through opera suddenly I was singing in Italian and German, I could sing Lieder because I understood it from my Dad. And it's those things you take for granted at home but when you're exposed to them in the real world you think, 'I can actually do something with this'. That's when my love of singing really flourished, and I moved over to the Royal Academy of Music. It really has been a journey, of moving between instruments, and understanding the instrument of the voice as well, and of collaborations with other musicians. For the very first time I found my community when I moved to London, and by the time I got to the Academy, I'd just found my tribe.

I went to see concerts all the time. It's quite humbling really – I recently hosted an event at the Royal Albert Hall and I could look down at where I remember queuing up for three pound tickets and sneaking in my food because as a poor student I couldn't afford the ticket *and* the food.

THE RECORD I COULDN'T LIVE WITHOUT

Holst The Planets
LPO / Sir Adrian Boult Warner Classics
The Planets was my very first introduction to a certain scale of classical music - I don't think there is a single composer that hasn't been influenced by it.

I'm a mezzo, and there's quite an excess of sopranos, and that's why I worked – I would get the last minute jobs: 'can you come and perform with Michael Crawford, he needs somebody who can perform on the radio, here's your music': bam. People will know me from Hear'Say, but my very first job on Top of the Pops was as a backing vocalist for Cliff Richard and KD Lang. That gave me a really good insight that if I could read music, and if I could understand what it is from a performer's point of view that people need, and fast, then I could work.

I'm working with a lot of content creation and my edits are sharp because I understand beats. Most people when filming will just try and hit a beat, whereas I bring a metronome and know I will *absolutely* hit it. It may be unconventional but these are music skills that I bring that I know work in other fields.

Music has given me a platform and I feel a huge responsibility to use that platform. When we went into lockdown I did music classes with my children – my sister in Australia rang me up saying 'oh I just logged on for these free music classes and it was you!' – and what was wonderful is my lessons were sitting next to Carol Vorderman and her math classes, and Joe Wicks and PE, they made this roster which was really powerful to be a part of, because we could spread the word about music in a way that translated it to so many people. We did basic rhythms, we'd show how an ostinato works, we were just introducing people where they didn't feel judged, and where children could just bring their pots and pans, or their trumpets, or their voices, and they felt part of the community. **Ⓖ**

Myleene Klass's Calm Classics is on Classic FM, weekends at 10pm

Sir Christopher Lee

Back in 2003, actor Christopher Lee reflected on an opera career that might have been …

My mother played the piano when I was very young. I never learnt to play, though, because my stepfather said, 'Playing the piano is for sissies. Let the boy learn to box!'

At Wellington I was a Greek and Latin scholar, which took up most of my time. Then the war came, and I joined the RAF. Though there wasn't really enough time to listen to classical music, occasionally it used to be on the radio. I became fascinated by Beethoven piano concertos and their wonderful tunes.

Then we were in Italy for two years, and the local radio broadcast operas: and suddenly one heard a lovely voice. I saw my first opera ever in the Teatro San Carlo in Naples, shortly after the city fell. I've still got the programme: it was *The Barber of Seville*, which is the opera I would take anyone to who had never seen one, because it has the most wonderful, catchy tunes and marvellous characters. Tito Gobbi sang the barber, and Giulio Neri, one of the great bass voices of all time, sang Don Basilio.

Back home after the war, I was one day in the bath, singing away in a very dramatic voice; and my mother said 'You've got a voice!' I told her about how I wish I'd learnt to play the piano. And she said to me, 'Well it's not surprising that you can sing, and that you now have this incredible love for classical music. You've inherited all of this from your great grandfather, Girolamo Carandini, 10th Marquis of Sarzano.' He was a singer at the Modena Opera House. He was also quite a chaser, quite a lad; possibly because of this, rather than the Risorgimento, he left Italy in a great hurry and settled in Tasmania. There he married my great-grandmother, who called herself Madame Carandini and became, before Melba, the finest soprano in the country. Their five daughters and two sons were born, as far as I can make out, either in Australia or Tasmania or in New Zealand. Madame Carandini must have been a strong character because she took these gorgeous girls who all became opera singers in horse-drawn wagons to out of the way places, including Queensland. They sang all over the world.

My interest in classical music soared to the point where I was a complete fanatic: mainly symphonies, concertos – Beethoven to me is God – but above all opera. I found out who were the greatest singers, and listened to their records on a wind-up gramophone. And I started going to Covent Garden; I saw everyone you've ever heard of.

Then in about 1948 or '49 I was at a party in Stockholm where everybody was singing student songs, knocking back the drinks. And I suddenly felt a tug at my sleeve; I turned

THE RECORD I COULDN'T LIVE WITHOUT

Orchestral Showpieces

NBC SO / Arturo Toscanini

RCA

Toscanini's music-making is absolutely remarkable for its clarity.

around and swooned slightly when I saw it was Jussi Björling: 'You have a real voice!' He told me to come the next morning to the Opera House and sing to him. I told him I hadn't been trained, but he insisted: 'I don't care what you sing. I want to hear the voice – the instrument'. I could barely believe this, but the next morning I stood on the stage, nervous as hell. And he was there, sitting in the stalls next to Joel Berglund: no piano – nothing. 'Sing something!' I did something unbelievable like sing Don Giovanni's Serenade. And there was a lot of muttering. I sang them everything that I knew from opera. At the end of it all, Björling offered to take me into training if I stayed. I couldn't accept because I didn't have the money to live in Stockholm. It's been the greatest regret of my life: I still believe I was born to be an opera singer. But then on the other hand if I'd sung professionally I'd have stopped 15 years ago at least, whereas I'm still acting. I'm too old to perform as a singer, but I can still sing. That's what's so extraordinary: it's because I haven't sung opera for three hours or whatever a day that I can still sing. **G**

Sophia Loren

Everything is music, the Italian star told us
in 2007: walking, talking, even acting

Because my mother was a professor of piano, you might say I was born in music. She played all the time, having gained her first diploma in piano when she was just 16.

I grew up in Italy during the war, and the only music I came into contact with at first was classical. Apart from my mother's playing there was only the band playing in the square in our little town every Sunday. Then, after the war, came the Americans and they brought with them boogie. So I developed a wide-ranging taste and now I can quite happily go from Mussorgsky to bossa nova and back again.

Unfortunately the only piano teacher I had was my mother. She was wonderful as a pianist – her Chopin was gorgeous – but not as my teacher. She was rough with me, every time I made a mistake giving me a little punishment! So I told her: 'I cannot study with you because you are my mother.' But we didn't have money for a professional teacher, so I didn't learn. I can still manage to play a little bit, but only like an amateur.

Yet that appreciation for music has never left me. Music soothes your nerves, it makes you happy. It is perhaps the only thing that gives me goose-pimples.

By a happy coincidence, I started my career in singing. My first film was of Verdi's *Aida*, although I was only asked to mouth the title-role. The singer was rather better than me … Renata Tebaldi. But I studied and studied that opera, and I was so much in sync that everyone thought I was singing! Years later when I had some success in my career, Tebaldi and I met and corresponded a great deal. She was very happy that I had done the film. She congratulated me on the syncing!

After that came another opera film, *La Favorita*, and this was really the start of my singing career. I went on to make various records, and as much as I enjoyed acting I adored music. There were some special memories; I remember having so much fun with Peter Sellers recording our comedy songs. Of course, music was a very important part of the atmosphere of a film. My husband, the producer Carlo Ponti, was not much in tune with music. I was the musical one. Whenever he got to that point where it was time to choose the music, he would call for my help.

And I am very sensitive to it, I feel that I can predict from hearing something whether it will work in a film. For instance, when my husband had to choose the music for *Doctor Zhivago* – and it had to be something that would both be popular and please the director, David Lean – I went with him to see the composer. I noticed a Russian balalaika and asked him to play it. As he played, I realised that not only was it very beautiful, it caught the whole sound of a culture that the film was about. And that became 'Lara's Theme'.

THE RECORD I COULDN'T LIVE WITHOUT

Tchaikovsky Symphony No 6
Royal Philharmonic Orchestra / Daniele Gatti
Harmonia Mundi
The *Pathétique* gives me chills. It is simply one of the most beautiful and moving pieces I have ever heard.

I couldn't imagine my life without music. And this has influenced my son, Carlo Ponti Jnr. He has studied the piano since he was a baby and is now a conductor. And it is a great joy to me that he has dedicated his career to finding the beauty in music.

As well as my son's concerts – of course – I go to as much as I can at the Maggio Fiorentino, where Zubin Mehta conducts. I love their choice of repertoire; it's very in tune with my personal tastes.

For me, everything is music. Walking, talking. Even acting is music. Acting is all about tempo and tone. If you don't get the timing right, you cannot convince people that the emotions you are portraying are real.

I remember one long speech I had to say in voice-over in *The Fall of the Roman Empire*, when Rome seems to be falling apart around me. This was one of the most difficult things I ever had to do, because it was like an extended theatrical monologue. I'm not naturally good at that kind of thing, so I approached it in musical terms. Little by little I found the tempo, the pitch, the rests and the pointed inclinations of the voice. And that's how I got through it. As I say, all is music! **G**

ILLUSTRATION: PHILIP BANNISTER

Dame Joanna Lumley

The actor told us, in 2004, about her love of Mozart's opera The Marriage of Figaro

The first music I ever heard was by Mozart; it was *Eine kleine Nachtmusik* played on my mother's wind-up gramophone in Kashmir where I was born. So Mozart has been part on my life for a long time and *The Marriage of Figaro* is a one of my favourite operas.

I think many actors love ensemble pieces – of course some like starring roles! – but I certainly love them. The first play I did in London was a farce and in a strange way not unlike *The Marriage of Figaro* (though there was no darkness in it – which there certainly is in *Figaro*). There's something joyous about the farcical nature of *Figaro* and in everything that is ludicrous in it, like the gardener with the bump on the head, people hiding in cupboards, people dressing up as others and being mistaken one for the other in the darkness. Yet all that romping only draws a thin cloth over the darkness of the women, all of whom I expect have been abused by the Count. So-called *droit de seigneur*!

And the Countess, who is so beautiful and lovely before, reveals the horror of being married to a serial philanderer. Not much fun! And Figaro, who was a darling, lively, chirpy barber before has suddenly taken on this really serious position in the household. He sees the ugly side of jealousy and feels anxiety about his wife, the nice, flirty, skippety, fun Susanna who seems to me to be what the Countess was like when she was young, and the Countess is a premonition of what Susanna might turn into. And maybe Figaro will get his leg over something lovely and flirty in the dairy when Susanna's 45.

This was brought home to me when I saw the Holland Park production this summer and Kate Ladner who was singing the Countess had, the last time I'd seen the opera, been singing Susanna. And this would be odd because our beautiful, tangle-haired voluptuous Kate was going to be the Countess and we all wondered – and I'm sure she did too – how it would go. And of course it was a knock-out but it had me thinking, wow, Susanna could turn into the Countess.

Before I was married to a conductor [Stephen Barlow] I just loved music but never knew why I loved it. Yet as soon as you learn about it you get more out of it. It certainly doesn't strip away the pleasure. It's like wine: of course you can enjoy it without knowing anything about it, even what it is, but the second you understand why you've got these particular grapes, or why it was grown in this sort of soil, and when they were picked, it makes everything so much more interesting. Knowledge enhances everything.

My musical tastes are pretty catholic but more classical than anything else. But into that is stitched big-band music and old songs from the 1930s – I sometimes think that I was born slightly out of my time. I also love music from the 1950s – I'm a passionate admirer of Doris Day's voice. In fact I chose her

THE RECORD I COULDN'T LIVE WITHOUT

Mozart Le nozze di Figaro
Soloists; Concerto Köln / RenéJacobs
Harmonia Mundi

I think Cherubino's 'Voi che sapete' is one of the most gorgeous numbers in *Figaro*, perhaps in all Mozart. It always reminds me of snowflakes in that it keeps to an exact form yet changes all the time. It's the most perfect geometrical form but so completely musical. On this recording the recitatives, which are done with fortepiano, are so exciting. The continuo playing is done with such spirit. The whole thing is like a draught of mountain water or a glass of great champagne.

singing as the theme music for BBC 4's *Book of the Week* reading the book I've just written. It's such a sublime voice and she can't hit a bum note!

I showed an interest in the piano when I was eight and so as a result I was allowed to take music classes. I still find that like telephone numbers which I dial wrong seven times out of ten, and writing numbers down (I always do them back to front), I found that I couldn't cope with the notes. I used to sing in the choir, but I'm not really a singer.

In my next life I'd like to be a musician of sorts. Actually I'd like to play the trumpet because I loved Eddie Calvert, the man with the Golden Trumpet for that bright sound that just cuts through everything. I also love the jazz trumpeter Perez Prada's playing. **ⓖ**

Cerys Matthews

How a Welsh childhood and early experiences of singing shaped the musician and presenter's love of music, as she told us in 2016

My earliest memory is of singing. A huge sow had jumped out of a trailer in front of us and hobbled down the country lane. What did we do but burst into song – 'Y Mochyn Du' ('The Black Pig'). It seemed my fate was sealed.

For every event in life there would be a soundtrack – every moment galvanised with music. Was I happy about that? I was obsessed. Music became everything, not just traditional Welsh songs, but music that varied from Puccini to Dylan, from *Cwm Rhondda* (we always sang at chapel, and always went twice on a Sunday) to Handel's *Messiah*. I was well and truly hooked.

There was always a piano at home, passed down through the female line from my great-grandmother – my grandmother was a mezzo-soprano, but marrying at 18 and the Second World War did nothing for her stage ambitions. I thumped at it in all moods, it was my best friend. And school? The jammy thing was being enrolled in a Welsh-language school, Bryn y Môr in Swansea. This meant music in every class. We sang in the bus on field trips, sang our maths times tables, sang as the seasons changed. We entered eisteddfods, recited, danced folk dances. Then the day came when a recorder was placed into my care. It was basically 'Three blind mice' and I was away.

Birthdays thereafter brought a different recorder model to my collection: fife, treble, bass, tenor. There were recorder courses back then in West Glamorgan, at a time when music funding wasn't threatened, and on one of these a teacher suggested I try out the oboe. Youth orchestra followed and became my gateway to heaven: added to that extraordinary feeling you get when a community comes together to make beautiful noises, was the off-stage camaraderie. My overriding memory, apart from travelling to London to play for Princess Anne at the Royal Albert Hall, is sitting, legs dangling out of windows of the Swansea University student digs where we'd stay. It was 1981, and 'Tainted Love' was top of the charts. We belted it out at full volume, the melody hanging in the summer air, then drifting out over the crescent-shaped bay.

I guess I've always been an advocate for the Duke Ellington school of thought: 'There are two kinds of music. Good music, and the other kind.' You can see this love for all genres and all eras in my weekly radio show on BBC Radio 6 Music. I'm a passionate advocate for sharing the best music available, regardless of the genre, of any hype or lack thereof, of what class, creed or tribe you belong to. I want to encourage people to keep their ears open, to judge it for themselves.

This has led to my involvement in the BBC initiative Ten Pieces, which aims to open the door to classical music for all

THE RECORD I COULDN'T LIVE WITHOUT

Purcell Music for Queen Mary
Westminster Abbey Choir / Martin Neary
Sony Classical
I can't get enough Purcell. Its profundity allows you to find new shadows on each subsequent listen.

schoolchildren. If you don't hear certain types of music, how will you ever learn to love it? Pop saturates our every waking minute. At its worst it's repetitive, unimaginative and insistent – it cannot compare to the palette of sonic colours offered by the wealth of recordings and compositions we have available to us. I want to set the balance right.

With this ambition in mind, my festival, The Good Life Experience, also features cross-genre artists and music. This year [2016] we are thrilled to present a UK exclusive of Max Richter's *Vivaldi Recomposed*, performed by The 12 Ensemble and Norwegian violinist Mari Samuelsen.

Classical music is a language best learned early, one we all deserve the chance to learn. Lang Lang is a shining beacon in this sense: in April he played for 5000 children at the Royal Albert Hall and, according to the interview he gave for my BBC World Service show, he has inspired 40 million Chinese children to play the piano. There's gold in them there hills, so give us Wagner for breakfast, we can have pop for tea! And in the meantime, just keep singing. **G**

ILLUSTRATION: PHILIP BANNISTER

Discover
a world of
music

With magazine subscriptions - whatever your musical passion

GRAMOPHONE
The world's best classical music reviews

Why subscribe?

Each of our authoritative titles bring you:

- In-depth features and news exploring your favourite music

- Exceptional new recordings reviewed by our expert critics

- Previews and concert listings for live performances around the globe

- Interviews with the world's finest performers and artists

CHOIR & ORGAN
Two worlds of music, one magazine

Start your subscription today

OPERA NOW

The opera lover's
essential guide

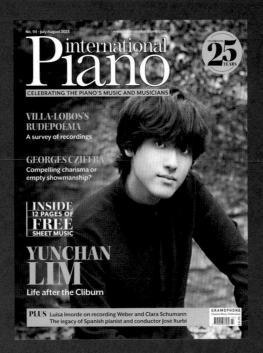

INTERNATIONAL PIANO

Celebrating the piano's
music and musicians

MUSICALS

From the West End to
Broadway and beyond

SONGLINES

The best music from
around the world

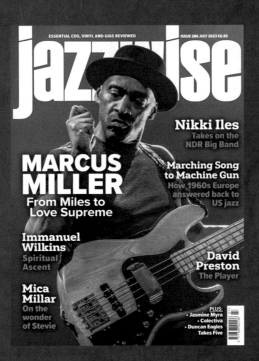

JAZZWISE

The UK's biggest selling
jazz magazine

MUSIC TEACHER

Your voice in
music education

Alexander McCall Smith

The author of 'The No 1 Ladies' Detective Agency' talked to us in 2006 about his late conversion to wind and brass playing

I started listening to classical music as a teenager in a very unguided way. When I was eight we had a wind-up gramophone, with the most extraordinary collection of 78s – I remember listening to Paul Robeson recordings time and time again. We then got a Pye radiogram, though we didn't have many LPs. I became tremendously fond of Ravel's *Boléro*, which I played again and again – you can imagine how awful that was for everybody else!

As a student in Edinburgh I discovered opera and followed Scottish Opera. My tastes then were largely 19th-century Italian. I hadn't yet discovered Britten, which I see as the change in gear of my listening tastes.

In my late 20s and early 30s I began to branch out. I shared a flat with Simon Bainbridge, who was composer-in-residence at Edinburgh University and who introduced me to new music. He played me a piece by Steve Reich, which I was really struck by, and that was the beginning of an interest in minimalism. I also started to listen to Maxwell Davies. I didn't explore in a terribly organised or well informed way. I tend to have stumbled across the music that I like, often entirely accidentally. Partly as a result my tastes are rather eclectic. I discovered a lot through the Kronos Quartet, whose recordings introduced me to composers I wouldn't otherwise have come across, such as Kevin Volans, who was on a disc called 'Pieces of Africa'. Over the past 10 years my tastes have probably settled down a bit in that I'm very drawn to music you'd describe as sparse and very pure – Pärt, Tavener, composers who send shivers down my spine. Poignancy is the quality I look for in music, a certain sort of loneliness, an echoing quality. I find that in the sadness of Celtic music. Barry Phillips, a cellist, does wonderful interpretations of Scottish traditional music. I've also recently been looking into composers who were alive in Stuart Scotland, such as Robert Carver. I do like church music. The English church music tradition is just gorgeous, one of the great glories of Britain.

We've got a very active recording company in Scotland – Delphian Records. I subscribe to their discs and there's great appeal in doing that as they're developing a really fine programme.

I am interested in so-called world music – though I find the name odd. What exactly does it mean? I suppose anything outside the mainstream Western musical tradition – but then it also includes Scottish traditional music. I'm interested in African music (though again the term is so broad it's not tremendously helpful – the music of Northern Africa is a completely different tradition to that of sub-Saharan Africa). I've been listening to music from Lesotho, a little kingdom entirely surrounded by South Africa. There's an extraordinarily infectious gaiety about

THE RECORD I COULDN'T LIVE WITHOUT

Mozart Così fan tutte

Soloists; Philharmonia / Karl Böhm Warner Classics
'Soave sia il vento' from Mozart's *Così fan tutte* – I love the sentiment behind it: 'may the breezes that carry you off on your journey be gentle ones'.

it. They use piano accordions, which I suspect came from French missionaries. It's absolutely amazing stuff!

I started to play wind instruments in my mid-30s, beginning with the alto saxophone. I continued to have lessons when living in Dallas, from a local instrument repairman who tried to teach me jazz; I couldn't play it, though he was tremendously tactful. I then started to buy saxophones from him, and bought the complete range. From sax I moved to clarinet, and then I thought I'd try double reed instruments and bought a bassoon. I recently bought myself a contrabassoon, a gorgeous instrument. I also took brass lessons, and did grade four euphonium. In the exam I played one piece in the wrong harmonic altogether, I was so nervous, but the examiner was so decent. I passed by eight marks which I thought was very charitable of him. He said 'it's so nice to see a more mature face at these exams'.

About seven years ago my wife and I founded an orchestra in Edinburgh for people who weren't good enough for the better amateur orchestras – often people whose children were in school orchestras and saw what fun it was, and felt they might have missed out. We called it the Really Terrible Orchestra. It's been a great success, and we've got more than 50 people in it. There's no audition. Some of the players are very challenged, others are really quite good but are all people who don't mind playing with the weaker brethren, which is marvellous. It's wonderful fun. **G**

Sir Paul McCartney

The legendary Beatle, singer-songwriter and composer in 2006 on crossing musical genres

One of my earliest memories is of listening to the radio when I was about three. It would have been one of the BBC stations and I remember my father pointing out to me the booming sound – this was the bass. He was a good amateur musician – there was music in the house all the time – and he would always be dissecting pieces of music for me and my brother: not in an academic way, but so we understood the components – the melody, the harmony. So I was listening to music as though it was a jigsaw puzzle from the start – it was great to be able to identify the different lines rather than letting it wash all over you. Analysing a piece of music like that fascinated me and maybe it's no coincidence I became a bass player.

There was a lot of piano music that has stayed with me, like Chopin and the *Golliwog's Cake-walk*. I really liked the play-out music of programmes, with the announcer intoning over the top: 'Orchestra conducted by Paul Fenhoulet', that sort of thing.

I wanted to learn to play the piano, but my father wouldn't teach me – he said I needed a proper teacher and somehow that never happened. 'Learn how to play the piano,' I was told, 'and you'll get invited to parties'. Imagine doing that now with decks or iPods! I did pick up the piano, by watching and playing around, and eventually I took over from my father for the family's New Year's Eve party. Everyone turned up in their finery, the girls drinking blackcurrant and rum or gin and 'it'. My Uncle Ron would come up to me and ask, 'Do you know *Carolina Moon*?' I'd say yes, and he'd say, 'Well don't play it yet!' He would wait and wait and judge the perfect time, then give me the nudge and I'd play it – timing is everything.

A lot of this light music had an impact on me as a composer – I took from it a deep interest in how to shape a melody. In fact, when I first met John Lennon you'd think we'd have talked rock'n'roll, but I remember us discussing *Little White Lies* – that kind of 1920s and '30s song was the platform we took off from.

I was 14 when my mother died and I wrote my first song, *I lost my little girl*. I only knew a couple of guitar chords but they were enough: I had the melody going up and the harmony going down from G to G7 to a C chord. It was a crummy little song, but it got me going. Since then, I've always been able to sit down and craft a melody. I start out with a blank screen inside my head and think, 'What kind of melody do I want? Where do I want to go?' And I reach for the piano or the guitar, either to use a sequence of chords that I know, or to experiment with new ones.

THE RECORD I COULDN'T LIVE WITHOUT

Britten The Courtley Dances from Gloriana
The Julian Bream Consort RCA
I still listen to a lot to Julian Bream playing Britten's Suite of Courtley Dances from his opera *Gloriana* – partly because it's on the instrument I know, but mostly because it's just lovely music, and Bream has everything

Composing *Ecce cor meum* was a great learning experience in that sense – it's much more chromatic than my previous classical works and there's a lot more counterpoint in it. I've done a lot of four-part writing before now, where the voices all sing the same thing at the same time. Using counterpoint to stretch the words became like a crossword puzzle. I hadn't realised that you couldn't just align the phrase with the notes and use fragments of it – they've all got to make sense.

I don't write to 'be' anything, I write to suit the occasion and I write for what I have available. Those of us who have made some kind of journey across musical genres may have led some people to classical music unwittingly, but the point to me is that there is a generation maturing with the music, who perhaps turn on BBC Radio 3 instead of Radio 1. They loved rock'n'roll, then Bob Dylan came along and the poetry became more important, then with Pink Floyd pop became more symphonic and it encouraged people to look to the left and right of what they were hearing. They started to want something more – in the same way that having loved Chopin in general I've lately got into the Nocturnes. What matters to me is whether the music is good, not whether it's classical or jazz or flamenco. All the great composers will stay around because what they wrote is well-structured. Maybe the avant-garde classical scene of the 1960s won't last in that way – like punk rock, it had to happen at the time and it made people listen again. **G**

INTERVIEW BY PETER QUANTRILL ILLUSTRATION: BRIAN GALLAGHER

Alistair McGowan

The impersonator and comic talked to us in 2013 about his love of classical music, playing the piano and singing opera

My interest in classical music started early because my parents were big listeners. They introduced me to Tchaikovsky's *Romeo and Juliet* and Prokofiev's *Peter and the Wolf* – and to Grieg. My father loved *Peer Gynt*, so one of my early memories was listening endlessly to 'In the Hall of the Mountain King' and, weirdly, 'The Death of Åse', of which I was a huge fan at the age of seven!

When I was little my mother got me piano lessons. I played for two years and was doing quite well, but when it clashed with football practice it seemed a bit wet when I could be outside running around scoring a hat-trick. So classical music went by the wayside until I was about 17, when I was watching Marilyn Monroe in *The Seven Year Itch*; the actor Tom Ewell plays the beginning of Rachmaninov's Second Piano Concerto endlessly on his record player. Marilyn's character asks, 'What is that wonderful music?' And I asked my mother, 'What is that wonderful music?' And she said, 'It's Rachmaninov's Second Piano Concerto. Let's go and listen to it after the film.' She had a Reader's Digest box-set of Earl Wild and I started listening to all of them. That was the moment: it's all thanks to Marilyn Monroe.

As a student I listened to a lot of Sibelius and even when I was writing comedy he would take me in a very dark direction. His Fifth and Sixth Symphonies have some really dark moments and a lot of surreal things I've written have been inspired by him. Then in my mid-30s I bought a very small upright piano and began fiddling around. For two years I was playing about an hour a day and getting really rather good at that sort of level – Grade 5 I was told. I was pushed in the direction of Eric Satie and now I'm trying to write a play about him for Radio 4.

I always found it difficult to find the time to practise, but when I was going out with Ronnie Ancona, with whom I did *The Big Impression*, she was infuriatingly slow at getting ready. It used to get on my nerves. She would say, 'I'll be another 20 minutes,' which was always an hour, and I used to think, OK, I'll just play the piano. It's a great thing to get over your anger! I was playing for an hour a day waiting for her. As the outfits piled up on the bed that were being discarded and chosen and the earrings were being discarded and chosen and the hair was being done, I was there learning Satie and Chopin and Debussy and keeping calm. When we stopped seeing each other, I stopped playing.

I took up the piano again last summer, having bought a friend's baby grand. Some new neighbours had moved in next door and we started hearing everything. To let them know how thin the walls were, I started to play, as a kind of warning to say, 'If you can hear this, we can hear you'. But the noise didn't go down, so now I just sit down and play – and I've got hooked again.

THE RECORD I COULDN'T LIVE WITHOUT

Granados Goyescas
Eric Parkin *pf* Chandos
This is something I'm never tired of hearing. They never cease to calm, soothe, inspire, comfort. They are just wonderful, wonderful pieces, every one of them.

I've discovered John Field, who I'd never heard of – and I've fallen in love with his life story and piano concertos. He's lovely to play Scrabble to. And his Nocturnes are very attainable for someone of my level. My fiancée Charlotte Page, who's an opera singer of some note – she does a lot of Gilbert & Sullivan and has been on *Friday Night is Music Night* several times – is in Toulon working on Stephen Sondheim's *Follies* so she's away for four weeks and my ambition is to get these two Nocturnes done by the time she gets back. She's much more patient than other girlfriends have been – but Satie said that money, like the piano, is only nice for the person who touches it. I'm reluctant to practise scales when she's around!

I once played a bit of *Für Elise* in a Posh and Becks sketch. 'He' picked up a cello and played the beginning of Elgar's Cello Concerto, which obviously was dubbed. But at one point I also played the big run from *Für Elise*, and of course everyone thought that was dubbed as well, but it was actually me! I've done opera too: I played the Mikado at the Festival Hall, which I directed for Raymond Gubbay. And the following year I played the Pirate King in *Pirates of Penzance*. The Scottish newspapers, who reviewed it when we were in Edinburgh and Glasgow, said I had a 'creditable' operatic voice. **Ⓖ**

Brian Moore

The former England rugby player talked to us in 2006 about how his love for opera developed

My parents had quite catholic taste musically, so I grew up listening to a very wide range of things, including a lot of classical music and opera. I never really took much notice of it, however, until I was trying to impress a girl who came to school in the sixth form. Her family was quite well off, so I took her to the Grand Theatre in Leeds for a performance by Opera North. As it turned out I enjoyed the performance far more than I enjoyed her company, which was completely unexpected.

Highly trained operatic voices are no longer simply voices to me – they are more like instruments. When someone with an unamplified voice captivates an auditorium of perhaps 3000 people, it's a triumph of pure human endeavour, which I still find more moving than anything else I ever hear.

I started off by listening to what people might regard as being the more accessible, 'easier' operas, such as *The Barber of Seville* and *The Magic Flute*. Now I find I've come full circle and back to them, after working my way through Handel and Massenet and dipping into Wagner.

Opera can be for everyone, so long as people are introduced to it in the right way. The principal question is how to get someone to a live performance for the first time. Sometimes it requires a leap of faith. I took one rugby player friend to see *The Magic Flute* and he was very sceptical. After he heard the Queen of the Night's aria live for the first time, he told me the hairs on the back of his neck had been standing up, because he wasn't sure if she'd be able to reach the notes. He now goes regularly.

It can sometimes go wrong. On the British Lions tour of Australia in 1989, the squad were invited to the Sydney Opera House. About half of us went along and unfortunately it turned out to be a performance of *Werther*. Half the lads left during the interval and, when Werther finally expired, John Jeffrey turned to me and whispered 'thank **** for that, he took enough time!' Even I had to admit this wasn't a particularly accessible first opera!

A lot of so-called 'serious' opera people seem to insist that you have to suffer as part of the art and I just don't understand that. I have sat through the *Ring* cycle and, quite frankly, it's like going to India – I'm glad I've been but, frankly, I'm not that bothered really and I don't feel any need to go again.

There is a clear parallel in modern novel-writing. I sometimes find myself thinking what hard work I am finding something and it's not because I'm thick or I'm not trying. It's just that great writers such as Flaubert, Zola and Dickens managed to write in a way that was easily comprehensible without compromising their genius.

THE RECORD I COULDN'T LIVE WITHOUT

Mozart Così fan tutte
Soloists; ROH / Colin Davis Philips/Decca
Hector Christie is a good friend, so listening to this reminds me of Glyndebourne in '98 when I spent the intervals relaxing in the Christie family home.

It's not *de rigueur* to like Gilbert and Sullivan and other light opera, but I've spoken to a lot of performers about this and they say the real problem is that it's so bloody difficult to do, because of the intricacy and complexity of the words and the discipline of the music. I like opera in English. I don't see why people should be made to struggle merely because the piece is in its 'purest' form in the original language. A lot of this was written for audiences in their own language, after all – it was meant to be understood. Opera wasn't written in Italian or German just to make it difficult for people.

I am far more interested in performers than in recordings. I have never met Bryn Terfel, but I would like to. I have seen him on stage several times, and I think of him as a real modern genius. What a natural performer he is – and he comes across as a tremendously gifted, hard-working and down-to-earth person.

At the ENO a while ago I recognised the name of one of the singers – Graeme Broadbent. He was in the same year as me at school, where he beat me in a singing competition. I was very annoyed at the time, but I don't feel so bad about it 25 years later, now he's turned out to be one of the country's leading baritones! I once did a programme about the ENO for Radio 4. I was surprised by how cramped the conditions were, and learned that, just like soccer players or rugby players, singers have their pre-match rituals and warm-up routines. They don't turn up and sing! **G**

Michael Morpurgo

The author spoke in 2007 about his fascination with the interweaving of stories and music

Being the vintage I am, it was on a gramophone, on records with a dog looking at you, that I first heard music.

My earliest memories are really about the story of music. My stepfather came back from America bringing with him albums of 78s; each one was the story of a composer illustrated by the music which they had written. So I knew the stories of Beethoven's life, and Mozart's, and Bach's, from these wonderful records. There were portraits on the front, and those are still in my head now – I've never forgotten the wonderful portrait of Beethoven. It was just a line drawing of the composer striding across a landscape, his hair blowing, his hands behind his back, birds flying over his head. When I heard the *Pastoral* Symphony, the part of it when the storm comes on, I remember looking at this picture of Beethoven and could just see how the music made itself in his head.

My musical talent was pretty limited, but I ended up at a wonderfully musical school – King's School, Canterbury – where I sang in the choir and listened to the orchestra. The standard was quite extraordinary.

My first concert (I would have been eight or nine) was very important to me. Malcolm Sargent used to hold children's concerts in the Albert Hall. I went to two or three and remember being able to lose myself completely and utterly in the music. They would play music with a story in it, *Peter and the Wolf* was a great favourite, and Sargent would talk to the children – he used to be wonderfully engaging. You certainly felt it was a very special evening.

The whole thing of stories and music is important. At school I loved singing pieces where a story was involved – I remember singing Mendelssohn's *Elijah*, the *Christmas Oratorio*, the *Messiah*. I just love the weaving together of music and words, it's one of those things I'm completely fascinated by. I do a musical event of my novel *Private Peaceful*, where I read extracts alongside this wonderful folk *a cappella* group called Coope, Boyes and Simpson, who write songs about the First World War, and sing songs by people like John Tams who is also doing the songwriting for the National Theatre's production of my novel *War Horse*. I love working with live musicians.

Mozart is still the love of my life. If I wanted to meet a composer, Mozart would be the person I would like to sit across the table from. In fact I've written a story about the power of his music called *The Mozart Question*. The genius

THE RECORD I COULDN'T LIVE WITHOUT

Tallis Spem in alium
The Tallis Scholars Gimell
It's unbelievable the way it transcends time and fashion. It is the most riveting piece of music.

of the man is that every time I listen to his music there's a freshness about the whole thing: it's almost as if he cooked it yesterday. It's also very personal, I don't know why, but I respond to the music enormously. To hear Mozart's *Requiem* I find the hair standing up on the back of my neck, because it's so exquisitely beautiful. It does not happen that way to me with other composers, even Beethoven at his grandest, or Mahler at his most grandiose, it's not so in tune with me spiritually. For someone who wrote as much as he wrote in such a short life, Mozart's compositions must have been unbelievably spontaneous, and I can feel the spontaneity – you could almost call it the honesty of the whole thing. I can never, never be bored by Mozart – even when it's played badly!

But there is a piece of music which manages to do something quite extraordinary, and that is *Spem in alium* by Thomas Tallis. That music, it seems to me, could have been written almost any time in the past 600 years or more, it's unbelievable the way it transcends time and fashion. It is the most riveting piece of music I know. I heard it sung in Westminster Abbey at the time of Ted Hughes's funeral, it was the last thing in the service, and it was unbelievably wonderful. I've never forgotten it. That's the last piece of music I want to hear on Earth – not Mozart but Tallis. **G**

Sir John Mortimer

The QC and Rumpole of the Bailey author talked to us in 2004 about his love for opera

My father once said to me that he couldn't imagine anyone actually liking music, so there was very little music in the home. As a family we never listened to it at all. But I was very keen on Radio Luxembourg and I had a little banjolele and the sheet music to lots of songs of the day – the words of which I still know 70 years and more later, even though I dare not sing them, if only because I can't sing!

As a child I used to perform all the Fred Astaire and Ginger Rogers musicals on our stairs obliging my parents to listen. I can remember going to hear *Elijah* at my prep school, but I really only got into 'proper' music at Oxford. My best friend at the time (who went on to commit a murder – but that's another story) introduced me to Mozart and, especially, Brahms's Fourth Symphony. That was my Damascene moment.

My other great moment came when I got a commission from *The Observer* to write about a week at Covent Garden – something I knew nothing about. That, happily, introduced me to opera: I saw Pavarotti there for the first time and a fine production of *Luisa Miller*. Going to the opera is the surest way to forget all your troubles – it takes you over completely.

My greatest experience was when I was asked to translate *Die Fledermaus* for the House in 1989. I found the discipline of finding the right word for the right note incredibly hard: I'd write a joke and then find it didn't have open vowels but did have badly pitched consonants and have to start again. But it was, with Thomas Allen and Carol Vaness and, later, Joan Sutherland, singing in it, the most rewarding experience. I had the unmatchable experience of taking a bow at Covent Garden!

I only did one other opera – *Così fan tutte* – and stopped there (some radio pieces aside) simply because nobody asked me to do another.

I was very much helped in my foray into opera – a daunting proposition for anyone initially – by a book by Peter Conrad which said that all that opera is is people singing their innermost thoughts, so it cuts out all the banal domesticity of relationships. It's why operatic characters can declare undying love for each other the moment they set foot on the stage. In reality, some of us choose to wait a little longer before uttering such unambiguous declarations!

I try myself to write prose that is musical, certainly with regard to dialogue which I think of as patterns of sound that mean something. In a sense my most famous creation, Rumpole, is an operatic character – a sort of cross between Falstaff and Fafner – who I allow to have his own 'arias'.

I'm musically conservative – I'm still very fond of Brahms, and opera stops for me with *Turandot*. And I'd rather listen

THE RECORD I COULDN'T LIVE WITHOUT

Puccini Tosca

Maria Callas et al; George Prêtre Warner Classics
I adore Puccini and I think *Tosca* is the best music drama in the repertoire in that the music tells you who the characters are and what the drama is.

to Classic FM – I find presenter Jane Jones's voice very sexy! – than Radio 3, although I have just discovered Shostakovich's quartets and concertos. But I am allergic to Benjamin Britten – there's something rather cold about his writing – and I have a total blank about Wagner. I fear he brings out the worst in people.

My other musical love is the songs of Gershwin, Rodgers, Porter and that wonderful generation of songwriters. The word was incredibly important to them and the way they used to just throw words away sometimes (which they surely got from WS Gilbert) is enviable. They were the great poets of their era and blessed by singers of the calibre of Ella Fitzgerald and Dinah Washington (who gave Noël Coward's *Mad about the boy* an earthy, strident quality you don't normally associate with his work). Now words mean nothing in popular song.

Currently I have a new life, because I now know so many rock stars. My best friend is Deep Purple's Jon Lord, who accompanies me occasionally when I give public readings. It's very satisfying even if I'm always being mistaken for the critic John Amis and wrongly attacked for reading scores during concerts and operas! **G**

Sir Andrew Motion

The former Poet Laureate talked in 2014 about collaborating with Sally Beamish on an oratorio Equal Voices, and about the relationship between words and music

Laurels and Donkeys, my loosely cohering series of poems about 20th-century Western wars, was published in 2011. One of the poems from that collection, *An Equal Voice*, is a collection of utterances by victims of shell shock, most of which were collected by Ben Shephard and are contained in his book *A War of Nerves: Soldiers and Psychiatrists 1914-1994*. But of course what I've done is to select them, shape them, top and tail them, fiddle with them a bit here and there, and generally to arrange them, to produce something which I think could be called a 'found poem', but which might equally be called a series of collaborations. I think provided you're completely candid about what you're doing with that sort of thing it's fine. But in my case it has very particularly got to do with at once showing sympathy, and not putting myself between the subject and the reader.

Sally Beamish has taken the poem and wound in here and there bits from the Song of Songs. I've always liked Sally's work since I discovered it about five years ago. I went out of my way to say to Sally, 'If you want to chop things up or rearrange them, do'. I've always tried to do that with composers that I've worked with in the past, the things I've written with Sir Peter Maxwell Davies, for example, which I started doing when we were both employed by Buckingham Palace. But it's always been that way around. I've never written anything for anybody after the musical event, so to speak, I've never written words to fit in with music; I've always written the words and the composer has come second on to the scene.

I've always very much liked the idea that music slows down words. Even when it's moving quite fast, it makes you concentrate on the words in an especially focused way. When you're listening to Britten – such a brilliant setter of words – set something that you knew previously without the music, the question of how much you're saying 'that's right' and how much you're saying 'that's surprising' is very interesting. It's usually quite a bit of both actually. I think Britten is probably better at setting words than most other composers I can think of. Purcell is very good at it, and I like William Byrd very much. In fact I seem to like English composers quite a lot, because I'm very keen on early-20th-century settings of poems. Gurney I'm very keen on, as a poet and as a musician.

When I hear my words set, I always feel excited and honoured, because I'm so interested in music without knowing a vast amount about it in a technical way, and I so profoundly think that poetry for me is a thing very intricately involved with what Robert Frost called 'the

THE RECORD I COULDN'T LIVE WITHOUT

Adams The Gospel According to the Other Mary
Soloists; LA Master Chorale; LAPO / Dudamel
DG
There's nowhere to hide in it, it starts at such a rate, and with such intensity. It's a wonderful piece.

sound of sense', almost a pre-verbal way of communicating its meanings. I know that my own poems begin with a pre-verbal musical ache which I then have to satisfy in some way, by finding words to go with it. But I think the relationship between words and music is innately extremely close for me. I remember a very beautiful setting that Tarik O'Regan made of a very short poem of mine ages ago, which I thought was absolutely lovely. He elongated sounds and phrases in it in a peculiar way, so I was a bit surprised – but actually my surprise was only a different way of saying 'how interesting'.

One other composer I'm particularly keen on is John Adams. Another absolutely brilliant setter of words, his setting of the Walt Whitman poem *The Wound-Dresser* is absolutely wonderful and the setting of John Donne's *Batter my heart, three-person'd God* in the middle of his opera *Doctor Atomic* is completely mind-blowing. John Adams is absolutely one of the people that I feel excited to be alive at the same time as, so that we can listen to these new things as he writes them and they come out. **G**

Rufus Norris

The Artistic Director of the National Theatre, in 2021, on music's significant place in his life

Many theatre directors would say that music was their way to the arts. Often, reading and imagining a play or building a production, they think about it symphonically, or as if it were a piece of music.

Music was pretty much *my* way in. My mum was a music teacher; she played the flute and the piano. I'm one of six kids and we were all born very close to each other so there's six of us within nine years. We had a knackered old piano when we were kids and you couldn't have your tea until you'd done your practice. When there's six of you, access to food is pretty primal: I'm a polite person but not when it comes to food … All six of us had two instruments up to at least Grade 4 and the piano was one of them. We'd end up playing in youth orchestras, often some quite big stuff. I never practised enough – I was always at the back of the second violins! Two of my siblings are now professional musicians and for five of the six of us music is still in one way or another quite a big part of our lives. Then I joined a band, wrote songs and so my musical horizons stretched from Sibelius to The Cure!

For seven years early in my career I used to teach opera singers how to act as part of a fantastic initiative called The Knack, which was setup by the Baylis Programme, the educational arm of the English National Opera. The course was run by Mary King, who is a completely brilliant person and one of the most influential people that I've had the pleasure of working with. In terms of my rudimentary understanding of opera, but more philosophically in understanding where the voice is rooted and how much it's connected to the body and the spirit, she was absolutely inspirational.

The great thing about working with actors as a job is that it's endlessly fascinating because they're all completely different. On the whole, even if it's not in an intellectual way, most of them are really smart and usually quite complicated – and I mean complicated in an intriguing, good way. Actors who have a lot of music in their background that I've worked with often are Rory Kinnear, Simon Russell Beale, Sharon D Clarke and Anne-Marie Duff. Simon is a really wonderful singer and when we're out of Covid I'm sure we'll get back to the stage where I'll be bumping into him as he sneaks in to The National early in the morning to get in a room with a piano, because that's one of his deep passions. His musicality and his wit as an actor is probably underpinned by an understanding – a conscious understanding – of the effect of changes in rhythm or even timbre which is drawn from the person that you're in a scene with. So if you're aware when you're picking up on each other's tempi or whatever, you define yourselves against that other person. There's a musicality in a scene: if someone is talking and slows down, there's automatically a change in the room because of what's happened musically. Nobody knows exactly what's happened but they know that something has.

THE RECORD I COULDN'T LIVE WITHOUT

'Iag Bari'

Fanfare Ciocărlia Piranha

I don't have any particular connection to the Balkans, but this music, which defies category, is unapologetically emotional and just connects.

And then, if they immediately speed up, there's an energy that's come in: the emotion builds, the air particles are moving quicker. With someone like Simon I think that's innate.

Orlando Gough is a lovely composer that I've worked with, and when we were building a show a long time ago, he gave me Fanfare Ciocărlia's 'Iag Bari'. There's something about it, partly because it's in a different language so I can't understand what they're singing, but the music has such deep, deep roots, and terrific energy and joy. It's completely theatrical in a way, a bunch of people round a family table or outside or in a concert hall, and it's very, very accessible. Of course it's only one step away from those extraordinarily beautiful Bulgarian women's choirs – the kind of stuff which I also love.

One of my most joyful times in the theatre was working with Damon Albarn on *Doctor Dee* for the Manchester International Festival and ENO in 2011. When music was being written, watching that process of creativity – being in the room with him just witnessing these things come to life in front of my eyes, with tunes which then will stay with me for ever – was fantastically exciting. I think if I could be born again I'd be a composer. **G**

Michael Portillo

How Wagner came to play an important role in the life of the presenter, writer and former politician – as he told us in 2003

My first experience of Wagner – a 1970 Coliseum production of *Walküre* – did not immediately win me over. It was not an instant passion. I'm not musically trained, and I don't think my ear was sufficiently adjusted. But I did realise even at the time that this was music and drama on an extraordinary scale. I have quite a memory of what the production looked like, with its huge spheres and ramps – a very dangerous set on which Rita Hunter performed with extraordinary dexterity!

It was quite a bit later that I was reintroduced to Wagner. I now travel quite a lot to hear music, but in particular Wagner and Ring Cycles. One reason is that I've had the good luck to get tickets – for instance to Bayreuth, which I've been to four times.

Another reason is that to go to a Ring Cycle is the most wonderful way to relax, particularly when I had ministerial office. Not only do you empty your mind of your normal cares but you fill it up with something else – with this story of dragons and giants and gods.

The plots are capable of limitless interpretation – for the composer there wasn't a single meaning, the concept changed enormously as he was writing it. So it isn't any aspect of the plot that attracted me, but the versatility of it, the limitless opportunities for exploration. The understanding of the human condition is remarkable. The range of moods and motivations that Wagner displays suggest that he had an extraordinary insight into the human condition.

Favourite Wagner interpreters? Two of my most memorable experiences are visits to see Reginald Goodall conducting the Welsh National Opera in *Tristan und Isolde and Parsifal*, in 1977. I have all of Solti's Wagner. And I love Birgit Nilsson, and am a great fan of John Tomlinson.

I've been to the Seattle Opera a couple of times to see the Ring. They are so proactive about finding an audience through a public education programme, and by making people feel that they have nothing to be afraid of in opera. And they manage to attract absolutely full houses. In the UK there's still a feeling that opera is for 'them', not for 'us'. Whereas my experience in the US is that there really is an attitude that opera is for everybody.

I think it is a widespread cultural difference. I remember going to a wine tasting in the US which began by telling you how to take the cork out of the bottle – which seemed rather laughable to the Brits, but the point is there are no barriers, no one is made to feel that they don't understand. And so it is with opera. You must throw the doors open, you must

THE RECORD I COULDN'T LIVE WITHOUT

Mozart Complete Violin Sonatas
Hiro Kurosaki *vn* **Linda Nicholson** *fp*
Erato

Linda Nicholson is a friend of mine, and I do love to listen to music played by people that I know. She plays the fortepiano, so it's a very light sound compared to what many people might be used to. It strikes me as very authentic, it has a vibrancy and an exuberance that I think is just lovely.

make people believe that there is no barrier, no first stage that they can't accomplish. Some steps have already been taken, including performances in the piazza outside Covent Garden, and the pricing of tickets in the Royal Opera House. Quite a lot is being done – and I think the next great area for further investigation is education.

In a way Wagner has become a pigeon-hole for me because I made a film about it, but it is not by any means my only listening pleasure. This weekend I'm embarking on what's become an annual pilgrimage – to spend a weekend listening to string quartets at the Castle Hotel, Taunton. The Lindsays are playing works by Haydn, Schumann and Brahms.

As for future plans, I can just say that it would be my dearest wish to go on making films about music and musicians. **G**

Dame Siân Phillips

One of Britian's finest actors told us in 2023 how music has filled her life from the very beginning as a young girl in Wales

The house where I spent my early childhood shook with music. My father played the piano every day beginning with Bach or Beethoven. Consequently before I knew what I was doing I could hum lengthy chunks of the more popular sonatas. It is said that Sir Walford Davies listened intently as I hummed the *Pathétique* on an almost empty bus to Swansea and pressing his card on my embarrassed parents urged them to contact him should they need advice concerning my future. I was five. They didn't. My promise was never fulfilled. I went on singing for my own amusement. By the time I was six I had a healthy repertoire of bass-baritone songs beginning with gems from *Judas Maccabeus* and *Messiah*, moving seamlessly through a little opera ('for thee a fond heart waits' I roared with spirit) and on into the parlour music of the turn of the century.

There was a wind-up gramophone which I was not allowed to touch but I sat contentedly listening to Caruso and Gigli, Al Bowley and the Don Cossack male-voice choir.

It was an intensly musical environment. Welsh children of that period played the piano and the violin, and their parents sang in choirs. My father taught himself to play the oboe and passed his piano lessons on to his brother who became a chapel organist. As you can imagine, in this society I was the Unmusical One. I hated piano lessons and the discipline I happily embraced where the spoken word was concerned totally escaped me when faced by a keyboard. But music had become an essential part of my life and I was fortunate to have encountered thrilling musical adventures.

Once, when I was a very young BBC announcer I toured with the BBC Welsh Orchestra (Rae Jenkins was the conductor). I wrote the scripts and met the artists at the railway station, timing the soloists' contributions. On one occasion, I watched warily as an evidently poorly girl rose from the floor where an assistant had been pouring oil into her ear. Still grimacing with pain she began to sing her number. The atmosphere in the little hall altered as we listened in awe to a young Joan Sutherland on the brink of her great career.

I have twice been lucky enough to join an opera company as they spent the summer months playing Noël Coward and Stephen Sondheim – so wonderful not to be microphoned!

Just once I shared the stage of the Albert Hall with John Wilson when he conducted *My Fair Lady*. On that occasion I didn't even have to sing as Mrs Higgins but it

THE RECORD I COULDN'T LIVE WITHOUT

Pergolesi Stabat mater
Emma Kirkby *sop* James Bowman *counterten*
Academy of Ancient Music / Christopher Hogwood
Decca

The piece I couldn't do without is probably Pergolesi's *Stabat mater* because it is a lasting memory of my beloved Pontardawe Grammar School and the pleasures of learning Latin and of being in a choir and much much else.

would be hard to describe the feeling of elation engendered on stage by this remarkable – and genial musician.

I think I am quite musical but I'm no musician. Nevertheless, music remains an important part of my adult life. Beethoven, Bach and Mozart are the composers I listen to most especially when I am performing. This is for pleasure but it is also a kind of medicine – Bach and Beethoven for grip and concentration, and Mozart for high spirits during a long run in a comedy. Never fails! **G**

Dame Patricia Routledge

How classical music has inspired one of the
UK's favourite actresses, as told to us in 2003

I can't live without music. My family was musical in the
sense that in my young days you made music around the
piano. Uncle George, Uncle Ken and my father would
sing the songs of the First World War and those wonderful
ballads that I'm happy to say Sir Thomas Allen has recorded
as 'Songs my father taught me' on Hyperion. Wonderful!
And he really honours them, there's no patronage.

At primary school in those days you would sing every day.
You'd have something called *The British Song Book* with all
the national songs of the United Kingdom. Then I went to
Birkenhead High School where music was very much
honoured and I also joined a church choir. At the school
there came during one year only an absolutely inspired
teacher, Miss Sleigh. She came for one day a week and took
all the forms right throughout the school and the standard of
class singing and appreciation of music just shot up. It was
quite wonderful. When she left the school and when I was at
University in Liverpool I continued to work with her. It was
a great grounding. I think she was very disappointed when
I didn't actually take up music.

I used to sing at concerts but I always found it terrifying,
really terrifying – much easier to hide behind a character or
play a role! This is why I have the greatest regard possible for
Lieder singers. It needs tremendous courage.

When I was at school we did an enchanting operetta called
The Puppet Show which was a very simple story but it was
based on the music of Tchaikovsky. So just as I responded
to poetry through the poems of Walter de la Mare – who
became much despised by the trendies – I responded to
classical music through the music of Tchaikovsky – who also
became despised by those people who think they have an
intellectual grasp of music.

So, after four years of university, I just felt that in acting my
facility was greater. Having a musical ear is an enormous help
though. Good writing is rhythmical, good writing has colour
and I do believe that singing lessons help the speaking voice –
they help the flexibility. I know we're not supposed to talk
about these things now because nobody bothers about them:
performances have become pared down because of the small
size of the television screen. But if you're in a theatre you
have to engage an audience for two and half hours and that
brings into practice all the vocal skills you can command.

I love choral music and as I get older I listen to more and more
chamber music but recently I've been listening to a lot of
Shostakovich. The first time I was exposed to his music was
when I came into New York after a tour of a musical called
Darling of the Day with music by Jules Styne and lyrics by
Yip Harburg. We arrived back a little bit battered and I went

THE RECORD I COULDN'T LIVE WITHOUT

Elgar The Dream of Gerontius
Soloists; Hallé / Sir John Barbirolli Warner Classics
The first time I heard *The Dream of Gerontius*
– a great, great work – was with Richard Lewis,
Kathleen Ferrier and Norman Walker. Amazing!
For a recording (and in a perfect world) I would have to have Janet Baker
as the Angel but on the Barbirolli recording the bass is disappointing.
Norman Walker would have been ideal!

round to a young friend for supper in his tiny little apartment
in New York. And while he was cooking supper he put on
Shostakovich's Fifth Symphony. I was absolutely knocked
sideways by it. I asked him to play it again straightaway.

I realised the other night at the LSO's Shostakovich concert –
the Second Cello Concerto and the Symphony No 15 – that
every second just told one so much. Shostakovich has extended
my listening ear so that I'm available to receive more and more
unfamiliar music. That's probably not a very profound thought
but he really has had that effect on me. His music tells the
story of the 20th century. I love those Jazz Suites – straight
from early film music. But there's all the pain and hideousness
of war and destruction. And yet there's hope and joy. Amazing.
And the Barbican was packed – which was marvellous. **G**

Robert Redford

The Sundance Kid and highly acclaimed actor and director spoke to Gramophone in 2008 about the impact of classical music on his work

I grew up in a – to dignify it – lower working-class neighbourhood in south-west Los Angeles. But, despite our surroundings, my mother and father danced constantly. They happened to be at the Ocean Park Auditorium when Benny Goodman got to the end of a tour that hadn't gone well. He told his band to cut loose and the result was the pivotal *Sing, sing, sing*. This was new, revolutionary – it was jazz rather than string band music. My parents carried that moment with them, so I grew up with music a big part of my life (my father's family were all string-players and taught music back east in Connecticut). I didn't play as a kid but was influenced by Goodman and the then ultra-modern Stan Kenton.

The transforming moment for me was when I was 15 and dating an older woman – of 20! She got me into The Haig, a small club in LA, a teeny, shed-like place across from the old Ambassador Hotel. 'I want to show you something new,' she said. It was a dark room with a lot of smoke in it, but everyone was wearing sunglasses and there was Chet Baker, Gerry Mulligan and Red Mitchell on bass. They looked weird, particularly Mulligan, who resembled a scarecrow. Baker looked like a teenager. Suddenly they started to play and it was like a spear running through me. It was a sound I'd never head before, and there, in 1953, I heard the new movement of jazz.

Later I went to San Francisco to follow jazz. I stumbled into a place where I thought I'd find some, and it was the City Lights bookstore. It wasn't jazz there, but readings of beat poetry. This was just as new, so the combination of these two original voices in two fields caught the mood for me and many colleagues of an era that was fresh and a culture that was reinventing itself. It was exciting and I hooked into it.

Aged 19, I went to Europe to study art. I was on the bum, travelling around and getting my education by simply being in the world, when I discovered classical music. I heard it in Italy and in the streets of Paris and slowly drifted towards it. I went to concerts of Bach, Vivaldi and Wagner, which was as fresh to me, a kid from California, as jazz. I responded to the depth and the feeling of it. Years later, when I got into film and had the chance to direct or produce my own, I could have a hand in the score. By that time music had a profound effect on me and I considered it deeply important to film, which is a collaborative medium, no matter who touts the auteur theory. So I drew on my own experience. Just before I directed my first movie I was in a place called Big Sur (California), which had a long, winding road in those days, of 65 miles or so. I'd decided to hike it, to understand its mysteries – this being 1962. I stayed at the Big Sur Inn, where, because there was a thick fog, I remained for three days and three nights while the road was closed. The old

THE RECORD I COULDN'T LIVE WITHOUT

Ravel Boléro

Anima Eterna / Jos van Immerseel Zigzag

The haunting, rhythmic insistence of that piece won't let you out of the room. That gets right down your spine.

Norwegian guy who'd built this shack played classical music every night while we ate and drank.

He played me the Pachelbel Canon, and it was absolutely haunting. When I got home I promptly forgot the name and never heard it again; it wasn't hugely famous back then. About 15 years on, I was in Big Sur working on a film with Sydney Pollack and suggested eating at the inn. The guy had died in the meantime, but during dinner I heard the Canon again. I ran into the kitchen and they told me its name. When I was directing *Ordinary People* I asked Marvin Hamlisch to use it in the move (he didn't know of it). Through that film it became better known (and I eventually got sick of it – suddenly it was played everywhere!), and I began to realise how big a role my own musical experiences could play in film.

Now I listen to as much classical music as I can. At the Tuscan Sun Festival I read poems to improvised music. There are plans to bring more music to my Sundance Institute. Classical music will always be around – it's survived time and fashion, and has far deeper roots than most types of music. As for Hollywood music, most of that originates from classical music anyway. **G**

Michael Rosen

The poet and former Children's Laureate in 2013 on his early encounters with music and collaborating with the Homemade Orchestra

My dad sang a lot when I was a child – lots of songs from all kinds of traditions. He sang English, American and French folksongs, German hymns, musical numbers … He was a classroom teacher but before that he was in the American army; he was in Berlin and France, and picked up songs wherever he went. He continued to do that throughout my childhood – he would hear a song and pick it up. I got interested in world music and collected African American recordings, and he would join in.

When I was 11 or 12, my brother got interested in classical music. He played records of Mozart, Beethoven, Handel and Haydn, and gave me a crash course in classical music in the process. He would read how a Beethoven symphony was constructed, and then put the record on, shouting out 'Recapitulation!' or 'Development!' His brain was bursting with information he wanted to share with me.

When I was growing up someone told me I couldn't sing in tune and I believed them. I would always say no to choirs and all that. I played records of course, but once Bob Dylan came along I bought a Marine Band harmonica. I kind of taught myself. I still play a little bit sometimes – 'Love it is pleasing', 'The shoals of herring' …

I've been doing a one-man show with my poems for 30 or 40 years now but I'd not worked with musicians until Colin Riley and Tim Whitehead from the Homemade Orchestra approached me. I said I would write something for them and they said, 'You're going to perform it, too.' I said, 'I can't count,' and they said, 'Don't worry – if you lose the beat, we'll bring you back in.' They set melodies to what I wrote, or improvised around them. We did the 'Nonsense' show together and now we're doing 'Centrally Heated Knickers'.

When I went to London jazz gigs during college, I didn't quite know what the musicians were doing. But working with the Homemade Orchestra, I hear things differently. Today, in rehearsal, the guy on the vibraphone played a sequence and I was supposed to come in after that, but, as I was saying to my missus, it can take me 30 times of hearing a tune to actually 'get it'. I'm either listening to the beat *or* the tune – the musicians are listening to both. But I'm getting better. There's a group of dads at the school my children were at and we've done several gigs together. There's a line-up of sax, bass, keyboard and drums, and they get me to do some poems. I can hear the drums when I'm doing the poems now – I know when to wait, when to leave holes.

THE RECORD I COULDN'T LIVE WITHOUT

Stravinsky The Rite of Spring
BPO / Sir Simon Rattle Warner Classics
I went to see the Pina Bausch ballet of *The Rite* and it was fantastic. If I wasn't so bloody busy performing, I'd see more of her work – and go to more concerts too!

With 'Nonsense' and 'Centrally Heated Knickers', we've gone into schools to do workshops. We'll start with rhythms and snatches of melody, which, for me, is a new way of writing poems. Tim taught these primary-school kids a beat and I said, 'Hey, look, we can put words to that'. It was something like, '"Go to bed," said mum". They banged out the rhythm with sticks, Tim played a melody – and suddenly we'd made a bedtime piece. Creating songs and poems is a bit like Lego – you have little chunks but you can build them into a whole sequence.

We've had some lovely moments with 'The Great Enormo'. It's meant to be a new way of doing *The Young Person's Guide to the Orchestra*. We premiered it at the Brighton Festival with conductor James Morgan, soprano Juliette Pochin and the City of London Sinfonia – and now we've got the CBSO doing it, too. I came up with this narrative about a futuristic theme park where you travel through time. We visit the Wild West and Manhattan, there's a pirate galleon fight from the 16th century … James and Juliette have composed a piece for each ride and at the end we put all the bits together. There's audience participation – it's a big piece.

I'm going to be narrating *We're Going on a Bear Hunt* at the Family Matinee Prom [in 2013]. I'll be jumping about and getting everyone in the Albert Hall to do the actions. I've done books with Tony Ross before but not simultaneous illustration like we're doing in this concert. I'm not daunted though – now that I'm a seasoned campaigner with the City of London Sinfonia, I can do anything! **G**

Martin Scorsese

In 2005, the director talked about his love
of opera and how music inspires his movies

I am certainly not an authority on opera but I did grow up listening to it. Or, perhaps I should say, listening to sections of operas or arias. Part of my experience hearing opera for the first time came through radio, and old 78s that my uncles had. For a couple of hours in our apartment before my mother and father got home from work my brother and I played these 78s. Many of them were Caruso and there were intermezzi from Mascagni and others.

My grandparents, who came from Sicily, only spoke Sicilian and would sing occasionally as they were working in the house – that was another way I heard opera when I was young. Besides listening to the old Italian soap operas on the radio, we'd listen to music on the radio and a lot of it was opera. Coming out of a working class background – and my family not having an education – television and film were key sources of entertainment. Television was simply *The Ed Sullivan Show*, and Patrice Munsel, Robert Merrill and others would come on and sing these arias and everybody in the room would just hush and listen to it. Of course it would be something from *Tosca* or *Madama Butterfly*.

People have asked me about my use of Mascagni's music in *Raging Bull*. Well, when it was quiet in our apartment and there was nobody there I would put that piece of music on. It was a vehicle for me, it took me to visual dreaming, so to speak, visual images – I imagined stories, I imagined camera movements. I didn't know I was imagining camera movements at the time, but I was putting stories together in my head to this music. And it touched a certain emotional chord. And there were other intermezzi, too, from other operas. But this one was really, really very powerful and then my uncles would play something like *Cavalleria rusticana* for me.

There's one aria where the character is singing about Lola in heaven, and if there's no Lola in heaven he doesn't want to go there. Well, that's *Raging Bull*! I thought of it immediately. I did not think of it for the opening credits however, but rather as a theme throughout the film. As Howard Shore, my collaborator in *The Aviator*, knows I've always been sort of fighting between actual scoring of a film and creating my own scores from music that I grew up listening to. So, I thought, I didn't have a score, I said well, the score should be Mascagni's *Cavalleria rusticana*, maybe the aria, certainly the Intermezzo, and then I got other intermezzi from *L'amico Fritz* and a few others and that became the score. And then almost by accident we put it on the opening title shot and it worked. It worked beautifully and set the mood for the film.

Music and film are almost one and the same. There's the rhythm, the pace of music – and the equivalent of that in film is the camera movement, how long you hold a shot on screen before you cut, if you don't cut, the look on a person's face.

THE RECORD I COULDN'T LIVE WITHOUT

Wagner Götterdämmerung
Soloists; Met Opera / James Levine DG
Wagner's music is an inspiration. Definitely
Götterdämmerung: at the end of *Gangs of New York*, it's 1863 and the whole world is coming down!

For me, actually, the editing process is really like creating a musical piece. Even if there is no music in the film – I think the shots themselves have a rhythm and pace. Most of the shots I design and most of the way I approach any scene comes from music. I usually put myself in a room or a couple of rooms for about eight or nine days with music and design a picture on the page. That changes, of course, when you get to location to a certain extent. But basically the philosophy of the shots comes from listening to music – all kinds of music. In *Aviator*, it certainly was jazz music and swing music of the '20s, '30s and '40s, but also Bach and Beethoven. Actually, originally we wanted to use the second movement of Beethoven's Seventh, but it's been used so much. But it had the right feeling.

Sometimes we play music on the set. At times we couldn't play it of course with a thousand people in the auditorium, but in *Goodfellas* and certainly in *After Hours* the last shot, the camera tracking backwards actually – the Steadicam rushing back – it's Mozart: one of his early symphonies, I think, and that was played on the set just to get the feeling, the joy of the music. The camera and the actors are dancers really – it's all choreography. Ⓖ

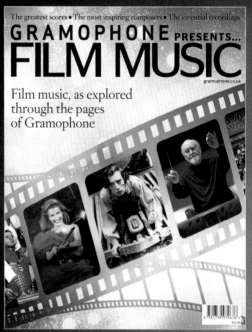

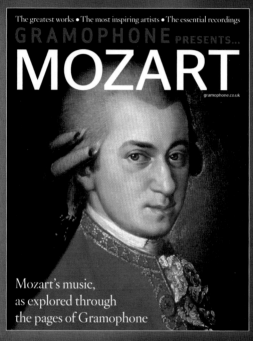

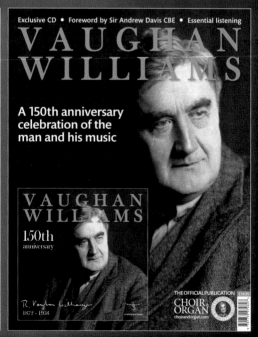

Vikram Seth

The award-winning poet and novelist in 2008 on the difficulties of writing about music

I don't have a very clear memory of it but my family tells me the story and I can imagine myself saying it. When my mother, who can't hold a tune, would sing a lullaby to me, I would tell her 'Mama, *you* don't sing; Auntie Kali will come and she will sing to me'. So clearly at the age of two I knew what singing in tune was – and I was utterly tactless: traits that have continued! To this day I find I can't listen to music when working – because, if I like it, then I completely lose myself in it, and if I don't like it, it irritates me beyond the point that I can deal with.

To me, music is more precious even than speech and words. If there are words involved with music fine and good but it doesn't necessarily mean that the music is dearer to me than instrumental music. I don't think a wonderful aria from the *Matthew Passion*, say, means any more or less to me than a Contrapunctus from *The Art of Fugue* which I also love.

For me the form for a book grows out of the context and, to draw a parallel with music, there are issues of orchestration. How you get groups of characters 'on stage' or put them off-stage yet not lose track of them. And how you tie things together in a large form … but on the other hand I might write a quatrain of four lines on youth or an octet on the dead. Each is 48 syllables – now that's a constraint. It's a constraint in miniature but it's a fertile constraint and it encourages me to think about things. With prose from you can't operate so tightly, but other factors come in. With my novel *An Equal Music*, why should it be written as a first-person narrative, whereas *The Golden Gate* or *A Suitable Boy* were written from a semi-omniscient narrator's point of view? Why should one be mainly in the present tense and one in the past tense?

I find writing about music incredibly difficult: it's hellish! After all, someone once said that writing about music is like dancing about architecture. There's also that fear of losing one's pleasure in it. And the whole thing can be undone by a lack of verisimilitude – if he's playing on the wrong string for example the violinist will be laughing. It's rather like those doctors who watch medical soaps and laugh because they'd have killed the patient if they'd given her that third pill! It's realism and you want to get things right.

In *An Equal Music* the quartet came in because I wanted Michael to be in an intimate group where there were complications and other dynamics, and a string quartet was ideal. I sat in on some rehearsals by the Vellinger Quartet like a fly on the wall. I found it fascinating how four individuals work together as individuals but also as one. There's no rules. There are some quartets where there's extreme acrimony and there are others where they're sleeping with each other. Of course you can have both at

THE RECORD I COULDN'T LIVE WITHOUT

Schubert Winterreise
Hans Hotter *bar* **Gerald Moore** *pf* Warner Classics
It goes to the heart. It feels as if he is not performing someone else's words and music but creating them as he sings out of his own desolation.

the same time! Also what *did* surprise me was how they ricochet from the utterly mundane – like underarm deodorant! – to something so profound like the transition from one chord to another and how to bring out the lines. How dedicated they are and yet how irreverent they are – that I found astonishing.

I adore Lieder. And Lieder virtually saved my life when I was writing *A Suitable Boy* because I couldn't sing Indian classical music as it would just bring me back into my book. But in Bombay there was an Austrian ambassador who played the piano and he said, 'Why don't you come sing Schubert?' I said I couldn't read music and he said just listen to it on CD and learn it by ear in the Indian way, and come and sing, and I'll play along. And we tackled *Die schöne Müllerin*, *Schwanengesang* and *Winterreise* and other stuff. It was just wonderful. ⊙

ILLUSTRATION: BRIAN GALLAGHER

Ritula Shah

The presenter of Classic FM's Calm Classics on the joy of listening to and rediscovering music – and of sharing that joy with others

I grew up in a home where music was really important, but not western classical music. My father was really into Indian classical music and was quite a good singer, so he'd sing all the time in the house and would listen a lot, so music was there as a backdrop. But when I was four we moved to a house in Harrow and our next door neighbour was a piano teacher, and her daughter a trained concert pianist, so whenever the doors and windows were open you could hear music. So from the age of four I was nagging my mother that I wanted to go and learn to play the piano. That, for me, was a really powerful memory.

I'm old enough to be lucky that I'm of the generation when music was still a really big part of state education. At primary school there was a lot of singing, and I was exposed to all kinds of music without even knowing it. There was a point where they decided that every morning as we trooped into assembly they would play a classical piece – you didn't even know what it was, but somewhere deep in your subconscious it entered and remained. But I really and truly began to understand music at senior school, which took it very seriously. I sang in the choir, we performed *Carmina Burana* and Mozart's Requiem. We were typical sorts of teenagers though, really – what we were interested in was pop music. I think, for me, it was a gradual awakening – though I think I probably did my best to bump it back down again! But there were really good musicians in school – you heard people playing Chopin to a very high degree for example.

At university I did a degree in Renaissance and Modern European History, and as part of that we went to Venice for a term. And, while I look back with a certain amount of embarrassment about this, we didn't listen to Renaissance music! I loved my course and it was incredibly rich being in the environment that you were studying, but it didn't occur to me until recently that we never really thought about the music. We listened to Vivaldi in a Baroque church because it was there, but we did it as tourists, we weren't pointed in that direction. But when I was watching the Coronation recently there was a piece by William Byrd which was absolutely beautiful, and I tweeted at the time, 'Gosh, I must listen to more Byrd'. There's this great gap, really – I haven't listened to much Renaissance music at all.

I would describe myself as 'Mrs Popular Classics', and I don't feel remotely embarrassed about that – if anything, one of the things that really made me want to join Classic FM is I really believe that classical music has become this thing that people think is complicated, and difficult, and 'not for me', and I would love to be part of a movement that overturns that. I want people to feel that classical music is for everybody. Elgar's *Nimrod* is on tonight's programme, and I know you

THE RECORD I COULDN'T LIVE WITHOUT

Elgar Cello Concerto
Jacqueline du Pré *vc*; LSO / Sir John Barbirolli
Warner Classics

I heard Jacqueline du Pré play as a teenager and there is a raw, emotional intensity that clearly grabbed me at that age, and it's never left me. It speaks to me at a deep level.

can deride it as a sort of cliché, but if you stand on those hills in Worcestershire, and you hear it in your head, you know exactly what he was getting at. Music is about emotion – whether it's Joni Mitchell or Elgar, or Chopin, or Fauré or whoever – it should stir you in some way, and I think it's making people see that. I think I'm very suited to my show: I'm sort of slightly romantic and a bit miserable in some ways, and those big emotional tunes totally play to me and my personality. As much as I enjoy cheerful music, I never got past that teenage angst phase I think!

It's an extraordinary privilege, when presenting my show, to sit there for three hours and listen to music. I think I'd forgotten about some of those Chopin nocturnes which I'd listened to in the past but not for a long time. I've started to go back and listen to Mozart more carefully too – I've realised that I really, really love Mozart, and again it's a really obvious thing to say, but having listened to so many different pieces over the last few weeks I've just thought 'right, I'm going to go back and listen to this properly, in a much more systematic way.' G
Ritula Shah's Calm Classics is on Classic FM, weekdays at 10pm

Fiona Shaw

The actor and opera director talked to us in 2013 about pushing young singers to their physical limits, meeting Hans Werner Henze, and being brought up in the 19th century ...

My mother was an obsessive opera lover who would play the piano and sing every night – and still does. She's 86, she's amazing, and her voice hasn't become an old lady's voice at all! I played the cello, but instead of joining the youth orchestra, I went to acting classes instead. I performed a lot. I was brought up in the 19th century in that my mother used to have musical evenings. We had a very big drawing room and people would come and play, so performing in the house was fundamental to my childhood and possibly to my professional life.

I used to go to the Proms although I didn't particularly pursue music – but my theatre friends began to be interested in music. Deborah Warner's first opera was *Wozzeck*, which I went to see a few times, and began to see that this form of theatre and music was actually very exciting. The thing we do in theatre is cut the air with 'moments', and of course *Wozzeck* does that a lot, where the music and the silence are playing a very high-definition game with each other. That's really what we're doing with Shakespeare or a classical work, we're trying to make the thing cut right through the air so that the audience not only hear it but feel it.

My other great friend is Phyllida Lloyd – she directed the *Dialogues of the Carmelites* and I found that devastating. Phyllida has this unparalleled gift at playfulness mixed with serious profound thinking, and Deborah has this austere sandblasting ability to clear everything away apart from the essence of the thing. One is a Roundhead and one is a Cavalier I think.

I worked a bit at the ENO Young Singers Programme, and I had great fun asking people to do almost impossible things – jumping off walls, or tumbling, or climbing whilst singing, and what was surprising was that sometimes they were better when they did something very strenuous. For all the huge gymnastic rigour and particularity of the training in classical singing, the thing I'm trying to do is find the personality of the singer, that added 'something' that is not just their voice, but themselves. I get excited when the singer is involved with what they're singing, when a choice they make is something that they emotionally recognise themselves.

When I did my first opera, *Riders to the Sea*, Pat Bardon was just delighted to be given the opportunity to play every Irish mother that she had ever witnessed or liked or disliked, and so her performance was infused with a sort of personal ownership that was beyond my direction. It set the bar very high in the room so that the others began to see this personal investment – it was very moving.

THE RECORD I COULDN'T LIVE WITHOUT

Britten The Rape of Lucretia
Janet Baker *mez* et al; ECO / Benjamin Britten
Decca
I'm directing this for Glyndebourne and I find it utterly mysterious - its disunities are really quite challenging.

When I started to work on *Elegy for Young Lovers* [for ENO in 2010] I couldn't understand it all. The music was quite difficult at the beginning – of course it became like mother's milk to me later. I went see Hans Werner Henze in Italy. He was just charming, this little mole of a man who climbed up from his wing-back chair. We sat down and had a marvellous conversation and he told me all about his life, and at the end of that day I felt I must put the opera on for him. Oddly your motivation is not particularly rational. He came to see it and we had cut one section of it because I felt it was too long – and he was furious! We did three-and-a-half hours of his opera and he noticed the 20 bars I had cut! But he was delighted by it overall, and wrote afterwards that it was his favourite version of it.

In some ways what I'm doing in the theatre myself is probably quite near opera, in that it's about the elevation of thought and speech to something that can become poetical. We're not trying to do realism in the theatre, we're not trying to keep the speech domestic – it may be the language that people use domestically, but it must always have an elevated poetical resonance in the theatre. You hold the thought and allow air through it – which is what the notes in opera are doing.

There is an audience out there whose mental architecture in relation to going to the theatre at all is probably proscribed by the super-realism of film and the hyper-ordinariness of television. We must just allow them the threads which are the human dimension, to encourage them to get on to the surfboard of opera. **G**

Paul Simon

The singer-songwriter in 2022 on memories of
Mahler and on working with VOCES8

My father's favourite piece was Mahler's Fifth, and periodically he would play it for me, and what I remember was the power of the full orchestra – it's almost bombastic, the way the brass and cymbals hit. Listening to it again it actually took me back to being with him, and him trying to make me become a Mahler aficionado. My own tastes when it comes to classical music are smaller – I tend to like Satie, and to a degree the Impressionists, Debussy, I like the flow of it, it's almost like trance music.

As far as making a good song, it's not necessary to have anything but just the gift that either occurs rarely or once in a lifetime – or more often with great professional songwriters. Take Hank Williams – his songs are very, very simple harmonically but they're very powerful, have very strong melodies, and their words are very relatable. They're great songs. Or the way The Beatles evolved from the early 'She Loves You' or 'I Want to Hold Your Hand', to more complex harmonic things that Paul did. Maybe critics would say 'he's modulating', but the analysis is unimportant – if the song is beautiful then it lasts. My music goes from pretty simple stuff like 'The Sound of Silence' – a very simple song in terms of chords and structure, but it might be the most lasting of what I've written – to 'Still Crazy After All These Years', which is more complex and has a key shift in the bridge that's interesting. Then there's 'American Tune', which really comes from Bach or before – that has a chord change on virtually every note.

I was driving along with my wife Edie, and we were listening to a piece and I said 'that instrument is beautiful, what is it?' It turned out it was a viola da gamba, so I looked up some pieces that were played on it, and one piece in particular was called *Canzonetta spirituale* by Merula, just for theorbo and viola da gamba. The viola da gamba was just playing two notes, but it was affecting the chord change, and the simplicity of the thing really captivated me. And while I was looking on YouTube I saw all of these examples of this group VOCES8, and immediately fell in love with them.

It was around this time I had a strange dream. It said 'you're supposed to write a piece called *Seven Psalms*'. I woke up the next day and wrote it down. Shortly after that I began to write little guitar sketches, and they grew into more developed pieces, and that went on for about a year.

I'd recorded the song 'Insomniac's Lullaby' with a few of the Harry Partch instruments, including the cloud bowls, and while there I had sampled them, so I started to lay the cloud bowls into the *Seven Psalms*. I was using them as overtones to the acoustic guitar, so I would pick out certain guitar notes, and add a certain spinning bell to it, but very subtle – it was just to make the track feel deeper and maybe dream-like. And I began to think, I wonder where VOCES8 would fit into this, and if they'd want to do it?

THE RECORD I COULDN'T LIVE WITHOUT

Mahler Symphony No 5
Vienna PO / Leonard Bernstein
DG
It's a very powerful piece – the complexity of the guy's mind, when I think of those internal voices!

So we had an afternoon in a church and began to look for places that they could sing, and there was one spot in particular where I was looking for a minor second sound in a chord, and I wanted to see if they could do it – which of course they could effortlessly. It sounded great. I tried having them sing words but that felt like an anomaly – trained voices have a different way of singing popular music. So I found I needed to have them singing *oohs* and *aahs* and closed chords, and quite often I would also take individual voices, mostly the sopranos, and add them to the end of a guitar note. What it does to the guitar sound is quite magical. You can't hear it as a voice – it just sounds like an extended ring. A few people I've played this for, they think it's a synth – it's so perfect.

Last summer I played a set at the Newport Folk Festival and I said you can donate my money to VOCES8's teaching programmes, which I support enthusiastically. Aside from their incredible musicality, they're very generous and very dedicated to teaching. We have a lovely transatlantic friendship, and I hope the story will continue. **G**

Wayne Sleep

The dancer talked to us in 2006, sharing his reflections on ballet, Boléro and Boult

Growing up in Plymouth, I wasn't aware of anything called classical music for quite a while. I always loved music itself, though. We didn't have a record player but in our attic was an old, broken 78rpm player which we'd inherited. I used to spin the turntable with my finger, holding the needle to the record with my other hand so that I could just about listen to Gracie Fields. Then, aged seven, classical ballet training included bits of Chopin, played very badly on an upright piano.

The big classical moment came when I was 12. I went to see *Sleeping Beauty* at Covent Garden. The overture started and for the first time I experienced the thrill of a full orchestra pounding out those incredible opening notes. I couldn't believe this sound I was hearing; it made me want to get up and dance in the aisles. Then I had to tear myself away at the end of the first act to get the last train home.

The music of *Sleeping Beauty* has always been special for me and has often marked important moments in my life. Two years after that first live experience of it I was making my Royal Ballet School debut at the Theatre Royal, Drury Lane, with the very same ballet. I wasn't the only one for whom the opening of that overture came as a shock. My grandmother came to see me in it and got the fright of her life when the great chords sounded. She was about 80 but jumped out of her seat and ran out through the aisles in terror.

I would sometimes appear for the Royal Opera. I danced in an *Aida* which starred Plácido Domingo and Grace Bumbry, and was Puck in Britten's *A Midsummer Night's Dream* with Geraint Evans and James Bowman. I often danced in ballet and opera on alternate nights. Everyone thought I must be the best paid performer in the company, which I wasn't!

I love the Russian school of classical composers – Tchaikovsky, Tchaikovsky, Tchaikovsky! Where would a choreographer such as Petipa find anyone to compose a great four-act ballet these days? Prokofiev and, particularly, Stravinsky free something up deep inside of me – they're both deeply dramatic, very unlike polite British society. Stravinsky brought folk music to the 20th century, made classical music modern, and that's very much where I come from. Showing how music matters and is approachable today is vital.

I've always given audiences a slice of classical music in my shows, alongside other styles. I used to do Ravel's *Boléro* as a pastiche of the ice skaters Torvill and Dean. The audience were suddenly allowed to laugh during a piece of classical music, and when they can do that they no longer feel it's anything to be afraid of. A lot of people think listening to classical music is like being in church, you're not even

THE RECORD I COULDN'T LIVE WITHOUT

Shostakovich Jazz Suites No 1 and 2 etc
Russian State SO / Dmitry Yablonsky Naxos
This is who I am as a dancer – crossing between styles. Some of it's almost like the classical world sending up more modern music.

allowed to cough. They often come up to me after shows and ask where they can get recordings of the music, and I send them off to the classical record shops.

In my early career at the Royal Ballet (I returned two years ago to tour *Cinderella* to Japan and New York) there was definitely a quality gap between the orchestral playing for the opera and the ballet. Most ballet conductors were not appreciated and the musicians would often send their deputies to do the rehearsals and even the first performance. But the next night they'd have Solti for the opera and they wouldn't dare do that to him. It made us ballet dancers feel like second-rate citizens. Although I suspect the players probably felt the same – in opera they can hear the singers and react to them; in ballet they can't see the dancers and so don't feel part of things in the same way. It's got better now, of course.

We did occasionally have big-name conductors for the ballet. The octogenarian Adrian Boult conducted me in *Enigma Variations*. Boult was so frail he couldn't make it onto the stage for his curtain calls and we all expected him to deliver a slow, lugubrious performance. But when he raised his baton it was like a bat out of hell! A lot of the dancers were left gasping. And he said to me, with a twinkle: 'Well my boy, do you want it faster?'. I love dancing fast so I eagerly replied: 'Yes, please!' But the others all said, 'God, no!' **G**

ILLUSTRATION: DANIEL MACKIE

Jon Snow

The journalist and long-time presenter of Channel 4 News talked in 2017 about how a love for music developed in early childhood

My mother, a pianist, was at the Royal College of Music and so there was a lot of music in the house. My father liked Beethoven and she hated Beethoven – so there was a lot of tussle about that! (She loved Brahms, by the way.) It was singing away with her at the piano that alerted them that I might have reasonable pitch and a good voice. As a result, they put me in for the trials at Winchester Cathedral and at the age of seven-and-a-half I got in. And so unfolded the most extraordinary experience.

I should have pursued a musical career but I wasn't actually musical *enough*. I could sing, and I could sing well. I had good tone, but the real problem was that I couldn't master an instrument and never got past Grade 3 on the piano and Grade 4 on the violin. And it was quite clear that I wasn't cut out for it. In many ways, it's gone to waste, except for my own enjoyment.

Our organist at Winchester was Alwyn Surplice – aptly named! – and he was a caring and decent man; he taught me a lot about music and a lot about singing. You'd have an hour-and-a-half of choral practice in the morning and then you'd sing Evensong in the evening – and that was on a weekday. Then at weekends you'd have three big choral services – Communion, Matins and Evensong – so if you didn't like what we were doing you'd be very unhappy, but I did. I felt I became part of the fabric of this medieval building. I'm lucky enough to have known when I was there that it was very, very special.

I have music on all the time, but I can't say I sit in a chair and listen to it. But it is very important to me all the same. I download music that catches my ear, but I'm not an assiduous collector of music. Even in the job I do, music is an incredibly useful concomitant. There are of course occasions when you actually need music to illustrate things and I know a lot of music that I can use. But it also provides a narrative – a narrative of the country you live in, a narrative of the Europe we live in. If you go to Vienna or Berlin, these are places where you want to try and locate the music.

There's that extraordinary thing that in moments of relative despair you will find people playing music – in Syria, in Iraq, in all sorts of places. I've come across the Syrian National Orchestra, 12 of whose members are here, and you suddenly see that for them that is a way of sustaining their 'Syrian-ness'.

I think this is the golden age for journalism. First of all, it's sorted the wheat from the chaff. The people who sat around at the back of the office and pumped out the occasional obituary have fallen by the wayside. But if you're up for it, in what used to be the conventional media, you've a fantastic future. Look at what we do: we put out a programme every

THE RECORD I COULDN'T LIVE WITHOUT

Vivaldi Recomposed by Max Richter
Daniel Hope *vn* Konzerthausorchester Berlin / André de Ridder DG

Purists may resist, but I must say I think it's a masterpiece. It's given me a lot of pleasure this year.

night, one hour long which about a million people watch. And you'd think that was it. But in this last 18 months, we've been posting elements of the programme in a format for mobile phones, with captions, and last year there were two billion views. That's quite something – more than any British broadcaster! And that's from a 100-strong outfit which has 15 people working online. That's got tremendous potential and I genuinely believe that quality will prevail.

I went to only my second opera the other day. (As a schoolboy, we were so steeped in choral music that we looked down on opera and I was never exposed to it.) I was on an Italian government trip to Venice for a seminar and they'd laid on Wagner's *Tannhäuser*. I worried about it because it took me up to such a pitch that not only did I cry at one point but I was completely exhilarated. Wagner clearly has the capacity to enable you to lose your sense of anything, except your emotions – and then to unleash them. (I worried a bit about what Hitler had got out it – and I'm still worrying about what Hitler got out it!) Ⓖ

Zeb Soanes

In 2014, the Classic FM presenter and author of the Gaspard the Fox books told us about his musical upbringing ... and playing God

We were a musical family. I was always told about my great-great-uncle, who was a gifted concert violinist who had moved to America. When he died, his violin was posted to us, in pieces. My grandfather glued it together in the shed.

Being brought up in the church – my father is a Methodist minister – there was always music around us. We would tour around little fantastically named villages with tiny, old-fashioned Methodist chapels with wooden galleries and harmonium organs. My mother would play the organ and I would read the lesson.

My mum was a member of the Waveney Singers, a local choir, when I was little. They were doing a Julie Andrews medley when I was about four and I would go and see them all the time – I briefly thought that my mother *was* Julie Andrews! She bore some resemblance to her and when I first saw *Mary Poppins* I thought that was my mum, so it came as quite a surprise when I found out it wasn't.

I had a fantastic music teacher at school who would play us *Fingal's Cave* or *A Night on the Bare Mountain*, and on the overhead projector illustrate the whole piece of music. We all had to copy the drawing while the music played. Even now when I hear some of those pieces of music I can see the pictures in my head. My teacher discovered that I had perfect pitch. When I started having piano lessons and my piano teacher put a piece of music in front of me which I knew, I would just start to busk it – and it infuriated her!

Very happily I've managed to use that early passion for music in my work now, presenting the Proms on BBC Four. It's such a privilege to watch an orchestral rehearsal, to sit in the Albert Hall in the afternoon and see a conductor take a piece a few bars at a time, and to hear the dialogue that he has – good or bad. And to get to meet people like András Schiff, or just to have a five-minute live interview with Vladimir Jurowski.

I recently played the Voice of God in Britten's *Noye's Fludde* in Lowestoft [Britten's birthplace]. The designer had said, 'Wouldn't it be great if Noah starts off listening to the Shipping Forecast', and the director suggested we should have me reading it. Then he Googled me and saw I was born in Lowestoft. It's the thing I feel most proud to have been asked to be involved in; working in my hometown was lovely.

I love singing when I get the chance. I get very grumpy when I go to weddings and funerals and people don't sing. It makes me really irritable because Methodists are known for their hearty singing! And I'm very much a traditionalist when it

THE RECORD I COULDN'T LIVE WITHOUT

Handel Dixit Dominus
Soloists; Les Musiciens du Louvre /
Marc Minkowski Archiv
When I listen to it now it just reminds me of a tremendous act of friendship, love and support.

comes to hymns as well; I love the old dissenter hymn-writers like Isaac Watts and Charles Wesley.

I have a very deep singing voice. I can manage 'Ol' Man River'. I was once holidaying with friends in California and we all went to karaoke. Because they were in theatre and film, they were all very confident singers. They got me up and I looked through the book, and the only thing I could find among the hundreds of songs which was deep enough was 'If I were a rich man' from *Fiddler on the Roof*. So we called it up and I didn't realise how long it is and how many verses there are! There are many ducks and sheep and geese and stairs in the middle of the house ...

I lost my voice last year for many months – I had a paralysed left vocal cord – and there was no guarantee it would ever right itself. I was spending a lot of time when I couldn't work contemplating my future and my friend Peter bought me Handel's *Dixit Dominus*. I would often treat myself to a long bath and a glass of wine, and listen to it in its entirety. The music is so beautiful. Really exquisite. Ⓖ

Zeb Soanes's Smooth Classics at Seven is on Classic FM, Mon-Fri

Juliet Stevenson

The actor talked in 2019 about how knowing about the lives of composers draws you deeper into their work, and in particular exploring Clara Schumann with pianist Lucy Parham

My involvement in Lucy Parham's *I, Clara* came out of *Beloved Clara*, which we've been performing together for some years, and which explores the letters and diaries of Robert and Clara Schumann. These projects, whereby the exploration of composers' lives throws light on their musical creations, are endlessly fascinating – of course, you don't need to know about a composer to appreciate his or her work, but to listen to a Robert Schumann piece having learned it was the last piece he wrote before being committed to an asylum allows you to be drawn into his music through an added lens. Lucy and I started to feel more and more strongly that, particularly with this year being the bicentenary of Clara's birth, she should be celebrated on her own terms – as a composer and a pianist, but also as a wife and a mother.

There are so many women across the arts who are chronically buried or underestimated, and I'm fascinated in rescuing them. I'm interested in the classical canon, but only if it relates to now. We like to talk about us being the first generation of women who've had to juggle things, but Clara had to do it all. She had eight children, she was teaching and performing, and she composed. I have to be honest and say that Robert's music reaches me deeper, but look, she had no role models when it came to female composers. Her letters reveal how she censored herself and was censored by others, how she didn't allow herself to practise her craft fully because her responsibility was to prioritise her husband's talent and look after their children. 'Marriage kills the creative instinct,' she wrote. If you look at what she had to overcome to be a composer, that marks her out. It's a measure of her talent that she was driven to do it at all.

I adore working with Lucy. To sit beside her at the piano, to see her hands on the keyboard, is such a privilege. Hers is a physical relationship with the music – what it costs her is astonishing. When you're up close, you see the sweat, the muscle power – she channels everything through the music. I've always loved working with musicians. I get a great thrill when I'm on stage with an orchestra – I love being the spoken voice inside an orchestral expression, and I love the combination of instruments and the spoken voice. I have long been obsessed with the rhythm of languages, which can contain or communicate as much as the literal sense of the words. All these factors – the heartbeat, the breath, the senses, the workings of the mind – fuse together to create rhythms which speak of an internal life. And this is what the spoken word and music have in common.

I'm the youngest of three, and for some reason my parents decided I was the musical one so I had to learn the piano from the age of six. A few years later, we were living in

THE RECORD I COULDN'T LIVE WITHOUT

Beethoven Spring Sonata
Yehudi Menuhin *vn* Wilhelm Kempf *pf* DG
When my dad was dying and we were nursing him, we played this recording a lot. The music has a lightness of touch, but it's also deeply profound.

Malta because my dad, who was extremely musical, was in the army and stationed there. We were at home and my dad was accompanying a clarinettist. Out of the sitting room came the sound of a clarinet playing what I now know was the slow movement of Mozart's Clarinet Concerto. I remember it like yesterday – I was frozen, I couldn't move. After that, I told my parents I wanted to learn the clarinet, but my dad told me I had to play the oboe instead. I accepted it and was grateful to him (he'd always wanted to play the oboe but never had the chance); after the first few months, I absolutely loved it and even now, when I hear the oboe in the middle of an orchestral sound, it still makes me shiver. I still have my oboe, but I don't play it, it's too depressing – the embouchure muscles aren't there now. I do sit down at the piano though – my dad's baby grand lives in our sitting room.

The speed of life has driven out music, in some respects. I'm on the run all the time, so I listen to less classical music than I used to. I might listen in the car, but my preference would be for contemporary vocal music. I struggle with opera though, particularly anything written before Britten. The music might be magnificent but that's not enough. I think Britten did for opera what Sondheim did for musical theatre; he radically reinvented the form, he infused it with a psychological intelligence – which is surely what any actor is looking for. **G**

Sir Patrick Stewart

The stage and film actor, talking to us in 2007, recalled his overwhelming introduction to the classical music world through Britten's works

Music played almost no part in my life until my early 20s. So much so that I worked in Liverpool for a year in 1963 and only years later did I discover who The Beatles were. That's how little contact I had with any music, and it's very embarrassing.

In my early 20s I became very friendly with a New Zealand actor called Rod, with whom I shared a flat. He introduced me to the music of Benjamin Britten. He put on a record of the *War Requiem* and – oh, it was overwhelming. We both sat there and wept. And with him I listened to just about everything Britten composed. If you're going to have an introduction to classical music, working your way through Britten isn't a bad way to start.

I was so ignorant about music that I didn't have any barriers to it or any prejudices. It was like the first time I went to Venice and nobody had told me that when you step out of the train, you're right there on the Grand Canal. So the shock of being one moment in a station and the next looking at that incredible scene was deeply intense. As it was, when I started discovering music, because I didn't have any expectations the stuff just hit me. Yet I did feel a natural affinity. Just as when my English teacher first put a copy of Shakespeare's *The Merchant of Venice* into my hand, and said: 'This is a play, read out loud. Stewart, you're Shylock,' and for no reason I could understand I just took to the flow of the sounds and the words, even though I didn't understand it all; rhythm and colour were things I'd also later experience in music.

I have always seen music in theatrical terms. During that first introduction I was working at the Library Theatre in Manchester, doing a new play every three weeks. That season I did *The Caretaker*, *Henry V*, *Twelfth Night* and *The Cherry Orchard*, playing leading roles in all of them. So I was awash in great writing and live performance, and my experience of music was very linked to that. My theatrical antennae were alert, and I plunged into the music in the same vein.

I came to opera in my 40s. I was living in Los Angeles shooting *Star Trek: The Next Generation* when I met Peter Hemmings, the director of the Los Angeles Opera. He invited me to see Maria Ewing in *Madama Butterfly* and I was so impressed that I went to see everything I could. Peter loved to invite me in to the Founders' Room, scruffy as I often was, having rushed direct from shooting, because he knew it was often something I was seeing for the first time, and he loved to wind me up and watch me enthuse.

One night Peter invited me to *Les Troyens*. I was completely transported by it. I was in the process of falling in love at the time, and the love duet will always be associated for me with

ILLUSTRATION: BRIAN GALLAGHER

THE RECORD I COULDN'T LIVE WITHOUT

Mozart Die Zauberflöte
Soloists; Vienna Philharmonic / Sir Georg Solti
Decca
The Magic Flute represents utter joy, playfulness and celebration of the world. You can't help but enjoy it.

that relationship. It also had an unhappy ending. If we'd stayed together there might even have been a funeral pyre!

I met Emanuel Ax at a dinner for André Previn (whom I have known ever since we worked together in the world premiere performance of Tom Stoppard's *Every Good Boy Deserves Favour*). He played gloriously for us all, and afterwards I heard him whisper to André, 'Sorry about that'. I thought this was so funny and so modest. We've met since, and out of the blue I got an invitation to narrate Richard Strauss's *Enoch Arden* alongside Manny at the Tanglewood Festival one summer.

We worked on it intensely, because it's almost like a duet. Manny helped to explain to me all the interwoven themes, and I found it all very affecting. We were cross when we did it in LA's Walt Disney Concert Hall last November because the programme notes wrote it off as a second-rate piece! There's nothing more annoying than sitting in your dressing-room reading that, just before you're about to go on to perform it. We've recorded it for Sony, and I can't wait to hear it and really explore the music.

I have worked with musicians at every opportunity. When I recorded *Peter and the Wolf* with Kent Nagano we actually won a Grammy. When visitors to my house see it and say, 'Who does that belong to?' it gives me great pleasure to say: 'It's actually mine!' **G**

Sting

The multi million-selling artist spoke to Gramophone in 2009 about how the barriers are tumbling between genres of music

Luckily I was educated by the BBC, when there was only the Light Programme and Radio 3, so you'd hear the *1812* Overture next to Kathy Kirby next to The Beatles – so you got the feeling that music was all one thing. Nowadays kids can listen to the same kind of thing all day – blues, heavy metal, reggae, classical music. It's all separate, ghettoised and I'm not sure how healthy that is.

My feeling is that music is a common language – obviously there's a difference between a folksong and Rachmaninov's Third Piano Concerto in terms of skill and application, but they use the same building blocks, so I've always had a healthy respect for classical music, and a desire to hear it and a desire to learn from it. I think that just by playing a Bach Prelude on, say, the guitar, you're sitting with the composer, you're seeing him make decisions. And with Bach you're sitting with a master – and *of course* you learn something! I can't say exactly what I've learnt (I can tell you what I've ripped off!) but that's what learning is. All composers steal from other composers. Bach is my favourite composer. People say he's emotionless but I can't understand that. I find him incredibly emotional – the Solo Violin Sonatas and the Cello Suites I just can't get enough of. I love them. It's the beauty of mathematics, which I don't find cold at all, I find it fascinating. It's architecture in sound.

More and more I feel the barriers are coming down between classical musicians and pop or jazz musicians. We've all been educated in the same kind of way. I had Daniel Hope on my latest album and he's a concert violinist but he knows as much about pop music as I do. And having a foot in both camps really reinforces the fact that it is a common language. I just did a concert in Chicago with the Chicago Symphony, an hour and a half of my own songs in arrangements for orchestra. There are obviously differences and problems. One is volume – they're so loud, the brass in particular! And the way we count time – symphonic time is very open-ended and expansive; it flows like the ocean. Pop music is very strict tempo, very metronomic. I kept watching the conductor and thinking 'Where is "1"?', and it seems to be after he's hit the floor! So that was confusing.

I know what an incredible amount of effort it takes to write a symphony, but when you make an album – an hour, an hour and a half's worth of music – you do have a larger form in your head. The way you select songs, the way they move from one to the next, key centres and so on. So it definitely rubs off on you.

That experiment with the Chicago Symphony was very interesting – and I'm going to repeat it with the Philadephia Orchestra in January. It's an interesting field and I suppose

THE RECORD I COULDN'T LIVE WITHOUT

Bach Solo Sonatas and Partitas
Viktoria Mullova *vn* Onyx
I have learnt so much from Bach and from these truly incredible works. They're endlessly fascinating.

orchestras are keen to get people like me to work with them because it widens their demographic. The symphonic audience is getting older, so I think it's important to broaden things without diluting what they do. To bring in a different kind of sensibility: that's the way art thrives and survives.

The *Twin Spirits* project [based on the letters of Robert and Clara Schumann, and available on DVD] came about through our neighbour June Chichester who raises funds for the Royal Opera House. The mission is to try and bring all levels of society into the Opera House – it's always being accused of being elitist, and there's some truth to that. But opera means work. And here in Britain we don't produce very much but we do produce art, opera, music. So all levels of the community should be involved, whether it's dress-making, set-making, and so the funds are used for that side of things.

The last opera I saw was Birtwistle's *The Minotaur* which I loved and the one before that was *The Magic Flute* – so the full gamut! **G**

Sir Roy Strong

Melancholy and grandeur reflect a unique landscape for the art historian, as told in 2003

I was entranced as a child by everything from Ivor Novello and Noël Coward through to American musicals. My father would have turned the BBC Third Programme off immediately, but he had a fondness for *La bohème* and *The Merry Widow*, both of which he took me to see performed by the Carl Rosa company. They must have hit me because I went back on a Saturday afternoon and saw *Madama Butterfly* from the gallery, amid the orange peel, and ended up soaking a handkerchief. I also saw the great *Sleeping Beauty* production which opened Covent Garden after the war; even then I wasn't so tuned into the music as with Oliver Messel's wonderful scenery.

I first responded to classical music through a record of *Sleeping Beauty* I bought after that production. I then played the flip-side, Rimsky-Korsakov's *Tsar Saltan*, and suddenly I found a tear running down my face. It was the first time I'd listened to anything like that, and I was utterly transfixed. While an undergraduate at Queen Mary College, London, I became very High Anglican; I went to High Mass at All Saints, Margaret Street, and heard wonderful Mozart Masses. I still adore church music: I've now got a curious role at Westminster Abbey as High Bailiff and Searcher of the Sanctuary. It's just wonderful to take part in those great ceremonies of state when the choir sings – what music!

I couldn't afford to go to the Opera House, although I *did* see from the gallery Visconti's production of *Don Carlos*. Then in 1967 I became Director of the National Portrait Gallery and began to go to English National Opera. They'd moved to the Coliseum, close to the gallery, so I had quite a lot to do with them: I gave talks, and when the scene shifters went on strike we sent a load of our frames over which they put on stage. I remember my first Wagner opera; despite everybody trying to put me off, I got a ticket for *Meistersinger*, crept up to the gallery at 5.30, and sat entranced.

Later, I married Julia Trevelyan Oman – I'd seen her designs for Peter Hall's wonderful production of *Eugene Onegin*. After our marriage we were into *Bohème*, walking the streets in Paris to see every doorknob, how everything was painted and whether somebody ought to have buttons or a handkerchief like so.

Through Julia I also married into Glyndebourne, where she did designs. She also did two of Frederick Ashton's greatest ballets at Covent Garden – *A month in the country* and *Enigma Variations* – as well as *Nutcracker*. So we went to all the ballets until I resigned as Director of the Victoria & Albert Museum in 1987 and started *la vita nuova* in Hereford. The odd thing is that having seen everything at the theatre for 30 or 40 years, we stopped going completely. And we don't miss it at all, although we have continued going to Glyndebourne.

THE RECORD I COULDN'T LIVE WITHOUT

Elgar Symphony No 1
LPO / Boult Warner Classics

I first heard Elgar's Symphony No 1 quite late in life, I think at the Proms. If I ever catch it on the radio I have to hear it all: I can't turn it off in the middle. I do find it absolutely emotionally draining. I don't know why: I think people read things into music; this seems to say something about the tragedy of England in the 20th century. It's got optimism in the end and in a way it comes through triumphantly, but there's also a terrible sadness to it.

I can't listen to music when I'm working. But when I go downstairs in the morning to start cooking I shove Radio 3 on. We always listen to the Proms. John Drummond, who is a great friend, used to invite us to his box, and we always made a point of choosing an evening with a new work. I've loved Peter Maxwell Davies's music since *Ave Maris Stella* was performed at the V&A. I feel his music has a pastoral, landscape quality unique to this country: Elgar, Vaughan Williams and Britten had it. And Tippett – if only he didn't write his own libretti! All their music has a mysterious, deep spiritual quality. It's not overt: the English are not very up-front about belief, but it's there, underneath all those layers. There's a melancholy. Grandeur, too: they can write coronation music and spectacle, and yet even that has a tinge of faded visions, insubstantial pageant. **ⓖ**

John Suchet

The newscaster, presenter and author, in 2008, on
how his passion for Beethoven's music developed

I'm a failed musician, I cannot deny it! I learnt the violin
and got into the school orchestra, and if you were in the
school orchestra you were allowed to have a
gramophone in your study, so I was the only boy in my
house to have one. Then I learnt the trombone. I won a
prize for it. I formed a jazz band for which I got punished
because the school wouldn't allow dance music, then I
formed another one at university.

But at school I'd made up my mind to go to the Royal
Academy of Music and become a professional, so I went to
see the school music director and he just said 'don't'. So I
didn't – and it rather grieves me to say he was probably
right! So I never took up music, although it was what I
wanted to do. I don't play now – I live in a flat so it wouldn't
be fair – but I'm in talks with a few friends and we may form
a band. Now that I'm retired from journalism I'd love to
have a crack at it. But it's really been about 40 years!

Music has always been in the background of my life, and
when I was an ITN reporter, globetrotting for 10 years, I
always had a Walkman in my pocket. When I was at school
I was completely addicted to Tchaikovsky. My piano teacher
said to me, 'You'll grow out of it,' and I thought, 'What a
patronising thing to say.' But actually he was right and I did.
When I started listening to Beethoven in my 20s it was as if
everything I looked for emotionally was there.

There's this image of Beethoven as a godlike creature with
laurel leaves around his head, looking stern and serious, and
yet I like to remind people that he was probably an
alcoholic, he had to find somewhere to live, pay his rent, he
had awful health, and if you met him you probably wouldn't
give him more than five minutes as he was so difficult – not
least because he couldn't hear what you were saying. And
yet out came this unbelievable music.

My Beethoven trilogy came about because I thought to
myself I'm not a musicologist, so I will try and write his life
as a novel. And in a funny kind of way you can actually get
closer to the man by fictionalising it, as long as you obey the
essential rules which I set myself: that everything that I
write about could have happened – and most of it did. All
I did was join up the bits we didn't know. I'm working on a
new book on Beethoven, on just the last three years of his
life. If you look at it in almost forensic day-to-day detail,
what is going on in his life is unbelievable: his health is in
complete breakdown, then you get the nephew trying
to commit suicide, his life was in meltdown – and in
between you've got the late quartets, the greatest music ever
written! Of no composer is it more true than Beethoven,
that if you know what's going on in his life you listen to the
music through different ears.

THE RECORD I COULDN'T LIVE WITHOUT

Beethoven Sonata Op 110 and Bagatelles Op 126
Jörg Demus pf Ars Musici
More and more I turn to the piano sonatas. This
recording was made by Jörg Demus on Beethoven's
last piano, at the Beethoven-Haus in Bonn.

A good performance of Beethoven should have you gripping
the sides of your seat. The knuckles should be white. I heard
the Lindsays play the whole cycle of quartets some years ago
at the Wigmore Hall – a rollercoaster ride. I was at school
with Peter Cropper [the Lindsays' first violin], two years
ahead of him. And the violin teacher said one day she was
going to form a school string quartet: 'Suchet, you're going
to be second violin.' And I said, 'Second?' and she said, 'Yes,
there's a new boy, he's going to be first violin and his name
is Peter Cropper.' In he walked with his hair, tie, collar all
everywhere and I thought, 'I'll soon see him off!' And then
we started to play … and oh, he was brilliant!

I think the greatest Beethoven conductor of the last century
is Toscanini. If you listen to his NBC radio orchestra
recordings – in the Eighth, the first movement under his
baton just catches fire. His tempi are all fast. He is the one
I turn to most often. ⓖ

Claire Tomalin

The journalist and acclaimed biographer, talking to us in 2009, on the legacy of her composer mother, Muriel Herbert

My mother, Muriel Herbert, was a composer and music teacher, and during the Second World War we lived in a house with three large grand pianos. I have fond memories of people practising Beethoven sonatas from that time and to this day I love being in a place where people are practising music. But although I had a few early piano lessons, and my sister and I would sing often with my mother, regretfully I didn't actually study music. If only I had studied a string instrument I would have been able to play string quartets, which seems one of the most terrific experiences you could have.

Recently there arose the opportunity to record a selection of my mother's songs. When she died in 1984 I collected all of her compositions with the hope of interesting people in her writing. Quite a few of her songs were published in the '20s and '30s, but when I showed her works to one musician he was dismissive. Then in 2000 Bill Lloyd, who had been a pupil of my mother's long after I was grown up, asked me to take part in a radio programme called *The Musical Side of the Family* for which he recorded a few of her works. I was approached again in 2007 by several different musicologists who were interested in women composers, and at that point Bill and I thought it would be good to record a more extensive selection of the songs. He showed copies to David Owen Norris, James Gilchrist and Ailish Tynan – three absolutely wonderful musicians – and they were enthusiastic.

Attending the recording sessions was an amazing high because half the songs I remembered and the other half I didn't know – these were songs my mother had written when she was very young, even before she attended the Royal College of Music. When I heard the Linn label had decided to release the disc commercially I was thrilled. I had hardly expected that, because the songs are very much of their time. However, I also believe that my mother had a voice of her own and that this was a true voice.

She had a great gift for melody and ideally served the poems she chose, setting them to music that was absolutely congruent. Some poets, as was AE Housman, are understandably reluctant to have their works translated into song, but there is a natural connection between lyric poetry and music. In my recent book about Thomas Hardy I point out that his father taught him the fiddle when he was a very small boy and took him out playing to people, so that he had rhythm and music in his blood from the very beginning, which must have been part of his formation as the great lyric poet he became.

Sadly, after marriage, children and the Second World War, my mother more or less gave up composing. I'm not sure whether her voice failed, which happens, or whether she was

THE RECORD I COULDN'T LIVE WITHOUT

Bach Goldberg Variations
Angela Hewitt *pf* Hyperion
Only one work? Bach's Goldberg Variations, which is to me about the most sublime piece of music ever written.

traumatised. She lived in a separate musical world inside her head and it is difficult to maintain that kind of refuge while being a wife and a mother and working at a job.

She left me with an intense love of music. I love opera particularly, and we would sing arias together at home. Perhaps it's a very romantic perspective, but opera's intense presentation of dramatic interaction between people, and also of private emotion, perfectly shows what human life is like.

When I was young my mother helped to set up a music society and we heard musicians such as the Amadeus Quartet, and Franz Osborn and Max Rostal. My taste is eclectic, from Mozart's *Haydn* Quartets through Schubert to Cole Porter. I have also listened to many recordings of French song, which my mother loved and sang often because my father was French. Debussy, Fauré and Ravel I find very congenial. ℗

THE STARS COME OUT FOR
GRAMOPHONE

ON OUR CLASSICAL MUSIC PODCAST

DECCA ICONS BERNARD HAITINK
with Rob Cowan

RACHEL WILLIS-SØRENSEN
on Richard Strauss's Four Last Songs

EXPLORING HANDEL
with Richard Wigmore

LAWRENCE BROWNLEE
on his new album, 'Rising'

RAFAEL PAYARE
on Mahler from Montreal

EDWARD GARDNER

ROSALIND VENTRIS
on 'Sola', a new album of music
for viola by women composers

KLAUS MÄKELÄ
on recording Stravinsky in Paris

KIRILL GERSTEIN
on playing Rachmaninov

LUCILE RICHARDOT
on Scarlatti and the songs
of Nadia & Lili Boulanger

BENJAMIN APPL & JAMES BAILLIEU
on their album, 'Forbidden Fruit'

RAPHAËL FEUILLÂTRE
on his new Baroque album

TIPPETT QUARTET
on the music of Korngold

STEPHEN HOUGH
on Mompou and his new book

JOHN WILSON

Simply search for 'Gramophone magazine' wherever you get your podcasts,
or visit **gramophone.co.uk/podcast**

Sir Peter Ustinov

The actor and director in 2003, the year before he died, on how classical music inspired him

My father was head of the German news agency in London, and made many friends among the leading musicians of the time. Before the War people like Schnabel and Backhaus came to rehearse at our home when on tour in London. Which is curious, because our piano was not even a Bechstein, but a baby grand Pleyel – in other words, a French piano, Chopin's piano. It was much softer in sound than they were accustomed to but they seemed to enjoy it. I was very shy, but would listen in and so got to know them quite well.

As a child I was really nervous – much more so than I ever have been in the theatre – and I was very nervous about having to play the piano at the end-of-term concert, simply because I find it very difficult to read more than one note at a time. So I gave up the piano as a bad job and took up the flute: there were only two bad flutes in the school orchestra and they desperately needed another very bad flute. But I had a very prominent upper lip, and the consequence was that I nearly always got the right note but usually in the wrong octave because I blew it at the wrong angle across the hole. Then I found out that I could 'do' the flute better without the flute.

I'm instinctively very musical and I can improvise vocally with all sorts of things. I do party pieces – pastiches based on quirks which I've recognised in various composers – which amuse me, but which have been taken quite seriously by musicians. People occasionally flatter me by saying, 'I shall never hear Bach in the same way now that you've done your cantata or your oratorio'.

My mother designed sets for ballet and theatre productions. She was very musical and knew Prokofiev very well: he was a student at the St Petersburg Conservatory at the time when she was a student at the Academy of Fine Arts. Her uncle, Alexandre Benois, held a salon with all the people who were involved in *Mir iskusstvo* ['World of Art']: Prokofiev was there quite regularly and was often asked to play. My mother became a great fan of his, and always referred to him to the end of her life as 'Prokoshka' – a term of affection which clearly existed from that time.

Prokofiev was always said, by Western critics especially, to be 'percussive' and little else; but I recently directed *The Love for Three Oranges* at the Bolshoi, and I was amazed by how lyrical some bits are and how they prepare already for the Second Violin Concerto. The start of my relationship with Prokofiev's music was really when I bought Heifetz's recording of that work during the War.

My first 'collaboration' with Prokofiev was when I was asked to do the narration for Karajan's *Peter and the Wolf*. I arrived and found the whole score waiting – Karajan had left long ago to do other things. So I listened to the music, and it struck me that Karajan had taken Peter's theme at a very, very slow pace: 'That sounds like Mahler!' I thought, and when I started the

THE RECORD I COULDN'T LIVE WITHOUT

Prokofiev Violin Concerto No 2
Jascha Heifetz *vn* **Boston Symphony Orchestra / Serge Koussevitzky** Naxos
I bought this during the War without listening to it. Then I practically ruined the record by listening to it again and again – I was so amazed by the magic of the slow movement. Heifetz is absolutely extraordinary, and it is an extraordinary lyrical achievement – the line is so long and so convoluted, turning in and out and back on itself; I listened to it in order to memorise it because I didn't want to let it go.

narration I couldn't resist singing 'Ewig … Ewig'! But then we played the music with the metronome, and Karajan's speed was exactly what was marked in the score! Anyway it won an Emmy, so I'm not grumbling.

What fascinates me about Prokofiev and one or two others is that they discovered a melodic sense which had never been used exactly like that before. I always had an instinctive feeling that the 12-tone system and all that is really a dead end, because you can't detach music from melody. I remember going to Humphrey Searle's opera *Hamlet*: it was all serial, and everybody was singing this terribly angular music. And then there came the extraordinary moment when Ophelia became deranged and sang the Willow Song: it was absolutely tonal, and extremely beautiful – you could have knocked the audience down with a feather. Then the whole thing was spoiled at the end by Claudius putting the music back on its serial rails again, singing 'She must be MAA-ad!' **G**

Rafael Viñoly

How a passion for music shaped the life of the late architect, as he told Gramophone in 2002

My father was the Director of the National Theatre in Uruguay at a time when things were going well in South America, so we were surrounded by a lot of touring artists who followed their European season with a tour of South America. It was an exciting time. We moved to Argentina later when my father worked at the Teatro Colón and we found one of those amazing piano teachers who seemed to populate Argentina at the time. She used to be one of the leading figures at the Conservatory in Florence and was an extraordinary teacher. She was very influential, not just in music: she helped me make my first connections with art.

The situation in Argentina and its political decay became really difficult so when I was about 32 we decided to move – without knowing exactly how or where. I left a major architectural practice and we went to New York. I had a very difficult time at the beginning; not quite sure what I was doing. A friend of mine said to me 'You've got to do something otherwise you're going to go completely mad.' It wasn't really the time when you'd go to a psychiatrist, so he said 'Why don't you go and buy a piano?'. And it dawned on me that it was something I'd always wanted, so I went to 57th Street, to Steinway, and bought a piano. Actually it was probably much more expensive than going to a psychoanalyst! But it was one of the best things I've ever done.

Making music gives you the chance to go back to true levels of aesthetic experience which are all too often confused in fields like mine. When you're playing it puts you in touch with a different kind of feeling, a different intellect and dimension. It's a wonderful thing to establish what it is to *really* understand a piece. Music is the only field in which you can't lie. It requires total honesty. Architecture is a little different. Many of the leaders of the profession today do not practise real architecture: it is a very peculiar phenomenon.

Buildings really are artefacts that need to be 'performed' – it's just that you don't perform them in the way that you perform a musical piece: it's how people use the buildings, it's how the buildings become ingrained in the culture, that's important.

Recently I've been completely engaged in the question of making spaces for music, having just finished the Kimmel Center in Philadelphia. It was wonderful to do because the first record my father ever gave me was of Beethoven's *Emperor* Concerto with Rudolf Serkin and the Philadelphia Orchestra. I think that the important thing about the way you work in buildings of this nature is that you must be capable of understanding conditions of performance that are not visual – there is not only the auditory dimension but also the mechanism of the relationship between the

THE RECORD I COULDN'T LIVE WITHOUT

Rosita Renard at Carnegie Hall
VAI Audio
I'm fascinated by the remastering of older recordings and a friend recently sent me a disc by this amazing Chilean pianist from 1949, Rosita Renard, who brought the young Claudio Arrau to Germany (they both studied with Martin Krause). Hers was a talent like a comet – she appeared, glowed brightly and then died and nobody remembers her. It's absolutely wonderful piano playing!

performer and the audience. This notion that you work *against* the proscenium is tremendously important: it is a notion that is completely architectural and operates on a particular way of seeing how live performance operates in society; this notion that you're in tails, I'm in jeans and there's this thing that divides us. I'm very interested in breaking that notion. For architects who are building concert halls, Hans Scharoun's Philharmonie in Berlin stands as a kind of icon. It is a real invention. It is a place that can only be the result of two people working together – Karajan and Scharoun between them came up with this building and because of that it remains unparalleled. People have tried to do this parterre effect but nothing has ever come close. It's really the first major step forward from a traditional hall like Vienna's Musikverein. **G**

Rufus Wainwright

The singer and songwriter revealed to us in 2005 a great passion for classical music

Growing up in Canada, you can't escape hearing a lot of Glenn Gould. So Bach's *Goldberg Variations* popped up all over the place, and my mother played them a little bit, too. At some late-night party one night, some drunken friend of my mom told me I had Glenn Gould fingers, so I listened more. I started taking piano when I was about six, but I was never very good at it. It took me ages to learn how to read music – I was really lazy! But in the end this really helped my pop career, because instead of writing scales I would write these melodies. I was more into Chopin later, when I hit puberty, but I still kept a 'healthy' distance from classical music as a passion. I find often with classical music it chooses a time to overtake you, as opposed to you choosing a time to overtake it.

Then something happened one night when I was 14 or so. We had gotten a copy of Verdi's Requiem for Christmas – the recording with Jussi Björling and Leontyne Price. We listened to it one night, and it was a religious experience. I was completely hooked, and mostly on opera at that point. The next morning I just started stocking up on Verdi. In fact, I would like to base my career on that of Verdi! Not so much because I think he was the greatest composer ever, or that his music is particularly cutting edge. I just love the way his career flourished, and how he managed to create this equilibrium between what the public wanted and what he wanted to convey. He seemed to struggle to not compromise either end of it. But what I also like is the fact that each work that he wrote was incrementally better than the last. I just love that snail's pace progression of just trying to get a little better each time. I also don't think there has been anyone who wrote melodies the way Verdi did – both sad and noble at the same time.

I'm also a big Schubert fan. If you're a song-writer, you really have to acknowledge Schubert as the father of song writing – and of combining lyrics with music. People have asked me if classical music has influenced my songs. It definitely has. In 'Foolish Love', I've been told the opening melody is very similar to that of the Brahms Violin Concerto. I didn't intend that at all. There is one melody that I ripped off: in my 'Greek Song' I took a line from a duet from Weber's *Der Freischütz*. I was always a fan of the *Four Last Songs*, and in some of my melodies you can also hear a lot of Richard Strauss's influence. Later on, I became more influenced by Mahler. If the world were to end today (and sometimes it seems like it is), it would be all right, because Mahler wrote his symphonies. I don't think anything encapsulates the end of humanity the way Mahler's symphonies do. I listen to the Bernstein recordings, and I love Georg Solti's Mahler, too.

THE RECORD I COULDN'T LIVE WITHOUT

Verdi Don Carlo
Soloists; Royal Opera House / Carlo Maria Giulini
Warner Classics
One of my all-time favourite operas and recordings is Don Carlo with Domingo, Caballé and Shirley Verrett (I'm a big fan of hers!). Verdi's operas are very deep, but they also have a pop sensibility, and on top of that, he had a great moral sensibility. He always has these deep meanings in what he was trying to say, especially to do with social justice and tyranny – I like that.

One of Solti's recordings that stirred my musical tastes was his recording of *Salome* with Birgit Nilsson. That was a big deal – I used to get naked and wear pearls and look at the mirror and listen to the recording. Recently I've been listening to an amazing recording of Berlioz's *La damnation de Faust* with Ozawa, to Brigitte Fassbaender doing *Winterreise*, and an old favourite, that amazing recording of Björling's *Bohème* with Victoria de los Angeles. It's really gorgeous.

I've been asked if I think pop music has 'taken' musical talent from the opera world, and I feel there may be even better singers than there used to be in one way, but not in another. Singers may be better trained today than they used to be: interpreting early music more correctly, or waiting for the 'proper amount of time' to take on a big role, and so on. But unfortunately in doing that, they lose a bit of their boldness. And you lose a bit of star quality that way because part of star quality is to be completely reckless. And I think that's more of what they're missing, that recklessness. It's a sad thing, in a way.

I think the classical-music scene has become slightly dormant, but one day it will 'rise again'! I just don't believe the explosion in the '60s and '70s that was pop music has wiped every other strain of culture from the mainstream. I don't know if opera or classical music will reach the heights it did in the 19th century again, but there's going to come a point where people just want to hear something good! Ⓖ

Sir Terry Waite

The humanitarian and author in 2005, on the power of liturgy and his love of Bach

I've always been an avid listener of the radio – our first family TV arrived in 1953 at the time of the coronation, but before that we'd depended entirely on the radio. On the Home Service there was a programme each midday, *Concert Hour*, when people such as Charles Groves and the Hallé orchestra would play for one hour until the news.

But before that, my paternal grandmother was very musical. She was, in her time, a piano teacher and during the depression in the 1920s, in order to eek out the family income she'd played the piano for the silent movies. As a boy of 10 or 11 I'd cycle the 20 miles to her house, and she'd play the piano for me. It was always her ambition that I should learn the piano but unfortunately we never had the resources to get one, and we lived in a small village where there were no piano lessons within striking distance.

I developed a love of music along with a love of language. I have that rather simple belief that good language and good music has the capacity to breathe a certain harmony into the soul. And that became particularly apparent to me during my time in captivity, when I had to spend almost four years in what was very strict solitary confinement, without books, without music, without conversation, often in the dark, always chained to the wall, sleeping on the floor. There I was glad that I had been able to retain in my memory something of music, something of literature. The fact that there is that construct of good language held within you, and also the remembrance of harmony and the balance of music, somehow enables you to retain a sense of inner identity.

This goes back to the rather unique combination of word and music that I fell into as a chorister – not in a grand cathedral, but in a very, very small ordinary parish church. Sunday by Sunday we'd sing the Psalms and the Collects of the Church, all of which had been unconsciously committed to memory. It's only later that you look back, and you can draw on that which you have somehow unconsciously learned, and recognise it has a significance beyond just repeating the words, beyond the music. 'Lighten our darkness we beseech thee O lord, and by thy great mercy defend us from all perils and dangers of this night' – a significant prayer when you're sitting in darkness. Somehow that combination that you had in the old Anglican traditional service of the wonderful music, the chants of the Psalms and the words put together, was a stabilising factor.

Our cathedrals – in the face of quite considerable expense, in the face in some opposition, and certainly at times with quite small congregations – are to be congratulated in maintaining that tradition which, probably unknown to them, contributes enormously to the backbone of our national identity. And all congratulations, too, to the BBC for continuing to broadcast Choral Evensong week by week. It must have been remarkable for the Lutheran congregations, where Sunday by Sunday they had the remarkable feast of a Bach cantata! Quite extraordinary. Bach

THE RECORD I COULDN'T LIVE WITHOUT

Bach Cantatas Volume 1
Monteverdi Choir / Sir John Eliot Gardiner
Soli Deo Gloria
Beautifully recorded, beautifully played and beautifully sung. If you want a good selection, this set is the one.

is so amazingly tuneful – he had such a wonderful sense of melody. I go swimming for an hour every morning, and as I was swimming today, going through my mind was part of the Bach cantata for John the Baptist, which is on the first set of the Sir John Eliot Gardiner Pilgrimage series. What a stupendous undertaking, to actually go around, as he did in 2000, and perform all the known Bach cantatas in the great churches of Europe.

I got a radio in the last six months of captivity. My cousin, who is a broadcaster – John Waite – occasionally would come on the BBC World Service and just get a message across from the family. Of course, they didn't know precisely whether I'd got a radio, and also they had to be careful, in case the guards were listening and heard them sending messages to Terry Waite. They did send a message occasionally in the last few months. And on my birthday, John said all the family are well, they all send their love, and they've chosen an organ piece to play for you. So they played part of Bach's Toccata and Fugue in D minor. And I was really quite moved by that, to hear sitting in the dark in that prison cell, not only the message from my family, but also that great organ booming out. And I thought there's a chance that one day I shall return to the UK and be able to go and listen to the organ myself.

One day I really must go to the St Thomas Church in Leipzig and the Bach festival. I should make that a priority. Ⓖ

Rick Wakeman

The progressive rock keyboardist and composer and former member of Yes talked to us in 2010 about his passion for Prokofiev

My father had an old radiogram and quite a large collection of 78s, including *The Barber of Seville*, which I thought was absolutely brilliant. Donkey's years later I did some concerts with the tenor Ramon Remedios of a fun thing that I called *The Barber of Wigan*, which was a pastiche of the clichéd themes and orchestral arrangements of light opera. I was stunned that people would come up to us afterwards saying 'we never thought we'd like opera, but we're going to go and see one now!' We'd have to explain that we hadn't really done proper operatic music, but it was great that it prompted people to try the real thing.

My father was a good player of all sorts of instruments, so he played the piano in the house, and there was classical music in my bones from day one. I owe my father an awful lot: he encouraged me to listen to and play as many different kinds of music as I could, and said to me, 'Classical tuition is the equivalent of learning to read properly, and it will teach you every technique you need to do what you want. An author can have a vivid imagination, but if he only knows 100 words then that will limit how much he can portray his imagination. If you have a thorough classical training, and also take the time and trouble to listen to and absorb other kinds of music – even if you don't like it – then that will let your imagination run riot.'

I studied at the Royal College of Music in the late '60s, a time when popular music of all sorts was stigmatised; but one of the saving graces was composition classes with Philip Cannon, who would give me a chunk of music by one composer and tell me to go away and rewrite it in the style of somebody else. That was tremendous fun, and it has stayed with me. In some of my concerts I play Beatles songs in classical styles: *Help!* in the manner of Saint-Saëns, and *Eleanor Rigby* in the style of Prokofiev – my greatest musical hero. When I was about eight years old my father took me to see *Peter and the Wolf*, which changed my life. I like to tell people that Prokofiev was the true inventor of the progressive rock concept album. I love the way his music can lead you down the path, and you'll be thinking, 'I've got no idea where this is going'; just as you're about to give up and walk back to the house, he opens the gate into a beautiful garden.

I've always been drawn towards 20th-century eastern European composers, and I adore English composers such as Walton, but there are also some weird things that I enjoy listening to. It's interesting to imagine what avant-garde composers such as Cornelius Cardew were trying to say. Whether I 'like' it or not isn't always the point – it gets me thinking that you've got to know the rules properly in order to break them successfully.

THE RECORD I COULDN'T LIVE WITHOUT

Stravinsky The Firebird
Boston SO /Seiji Ozawa Seraphim
I imagine it was a perfect day for everybody involved when they recorded that – it must have felt absolutely spot-on.

The Mellotron was an appalling instrument, often violently out of tune, but it was an innovation back in the early '70s, and it had a choir-type sound. Just for a bit of tongue-in-cheek fun during a sound-check for a Yes gig, I played a burst of the 'Hallelujah' chorus on one, and the band all said that I should put it into the show. On the first night that we did it, in front of about 20,000 people, I realised how astonishing it is that every single person knows that particular theme, even if they've never listened to *Messiah*. It's also heartwarming that thousands of Yes fans were turned on to Stravinsky because we used the finale from the *The Firebird* as the introduction music to our shows. In fact, there were phenomenal complaints when we stopped using it for a short while, and it had to be reinstated! Jon Anderson and I sat through about 20 different recordings before we found one by Seiji Ozawa and the Boston Symphony Orchestra that pulls out all of the different emotions and dramatic colours in the music. I've got about 12 versions on CD now, but that is certainly still the one for me. **G**

INTERVIEW BY DAVID VICKERS ILLUSTRATION: KEVIN SPENCER

Sir Derek Walcott

The Nobel Prize-winning poet talked to us in 2008 about opera writing, and the melody that infuses Caribbean speech

Classical music was there when I was growing up in Saint Lucia and there was a pretty high level of experience. Some people would perform it privately; in particular traditional English songs were sung. And classical was not strange to any of us because it was played a lot at school and college and many of us were exposed to the strong choral traditions in the Caribbean (though I didn't sing).

The context for all that though was a great mix of all different kinds of music. There were the local rhythms, calypso, zouk music. A great deal of Spanish and French-influenced music. That was the background. I learnt to move between different musical styles.

When I went to university in Jamaica, the professor asked me what I liked, and I replied, '*Dance of the Hours*, and *Les Sylphides*'. I thought I was talking on a very high plane! So, as I quickly discovered, I didn't have any thorough knowledge at all. Even if my knowledge is limited, in terms of appreciation, Mozart swings! We understand that in the Caribbean. The brightness, vivacity – and that goes for Bach too. We assimilate this music into our own traditions. To hear a steel band playing these classics can be terrific.

Beyond music itself, though, melody in speech in the Caribbean is very strong – at times so strong that it is incoherent. It is felt very deeply and has its own melody in me. In the Caribbean we often parody that speech melody in our music, simply by following the tunes of the language. I'm a Caribbean writer and everything that goes with the Caribbean Islands goes with me – strong melody, a deep sense of rhythm, all this is part of my nature. Some allegedly 'advanced' cultures look at these traditions and shun them. I've had students in the US, for instance, say that they don't want to work with ideas of melody because it can't work for them. So they don't use rhyme in their writing, structure as an idea borne out of rhythm they see as old-fashioned.

In the Caribbean, being 'old-fashioned' is considered a good thing. Harmony, rhythm, shape, they are all there in our novels and plays as well as our music. What has happened culturally elsewhere seems to me almost disastrous – when I see two squiggles and am told it is a painting. Many of my students find it very hard to write a sonnet, again because they feel that ideas of structure are old-fashioned. They look at the likes of William Carlos Williams and say that he brought freedom to writing. In fact he was a fine structural talent and he did the opposite, imposing a very strict monosyllabic discipline to what he was writing.

Yet this idea of anything being 'classical' in the Caribbean doesn't really exist, because you have to be backward as an

THE RECORD I COULDN'T LIVE WITHOUT

Bach Jesu, Joy of Man's Desiring
Myra Hess *pf*
Biddulph

I adore this work, because of its simplicity. In many of its qualities it is very West Indian.

artist. There's nothing unusual about this; Picasso wasn't avant-garde, he would say himself that he was old-fashioned.

Going back to your roots isn't an academic notion, it's a real thing. I wrote a version of *The Odyssey*, and the approach to Capri is physically quite similar to that at Saint Lucia. So coming home each time I have something of the same experience that Odysseus might have had seeing his homeland from the sea. Beginnings last, they are important. That's why Bach works, whether on a steel band or played by a modern orchestra – he was the beginning of so much.

I'm working with a fellow poet, Seamus Heaney, on my first opera project, *The Burial at Thebes*, to be staged at Shakespeare's Globe in London, among other places, in October. I will be directing, Dominique Le Gendre will be composing. I want to see from the inside what happens when great language and great music join – how can you get to that level of radiance? In opera the poetry is not the only thing that counts. But since there is poetry in music, and music in poetry, it will be an entirely natural alliance. **G**

ILLUSTRATION: BRIAN GALLAGHER

Sir Tim Waterstone

The founder of the bookshop chain, talking in 2019, on discovering Rachmaninov – and on singing along to Vaughan Williams in the car!

I grew up in a completely unmusical family, no books, no music, but I went to boarding school very early – aged just six – and tried to learn the piano, and it gave me an interest in, and curiosity about, classical music. In the village was a music shop and I wandered in there one day. LPs had just come on the market – so about 1948 – and I was just poking around and the kindly owner of the shop asked what I was looking for. I said I didn't really know, I explained I played the piano a bit and was fascinated to learn more about what classical music was. So he said, 'How much money have you got?' and I said, 'None whatsoever'. So he said: 'What I'll do is I'll give you a scratched LP from the back of the shop, and if you like that, come back and I'll give you another one.' My mother was out, and so I put it on the radiogram and opened up the French windows into our garden and sat there, and this music burst forth, and it was a total, total revelation to me. It was a fantastic moment – I had absolutely no idea that classical music could be so beautiful. I'd been given the perfect choice for a child of that age – Rachmaninov's Second Piano Concerto with the Liverpool Philharmonic, and Cyril Smith the soloist. I just absolutely adored it, and kept on playing it and playing it.

I'm not really a chamber music man – I love the big concertos, the big symphonies, but I particularly love the human voice, and sacred music very much, big Masses and Requiems and oratorios. Verdi, Fauré, Schubert – I just absolutely love it, it reaches a part of me, dare I say, partly spiritual, partly artistic. And opera – I love the music but don't really love the theatre of it at all actually. Just over my coffee half an hour ago I played the wonderful Dame Eva Turner singing 'In questa reggia' from *Turandot* – gosh, shivers go down my back no matter how many times I hear that.

I love Elgar's *Dream of Gerontius*, an absolutely sublime oratorio – and Janet Baker was my choice for BBC's *Desert Island Discs*. I just love Janet Baker's voice – I only found out a couple of years ago that she'd started as a contralto then moved up into the mezzo repertoire, but there's something about the contralto left in her voice, that chocolatey quality. Much of Elgar resonates with me. I love both the symphonies (I actually prefer the Second to the First I think) and the Cello Concerto – it's lovely seeing it coming through to be really played throughout the world now.

I also love Goldmark's Violin Concerto, particularly the slow movement. So many wonderful soloists have tried to get the piece into the repertoire and yet it's never really worked. Itzhak Perlman tried very hard, with André Previn, in the 1970s, and Joshua Bell had a go at it, but nobody's succeeded. But it is so beautiful. I first encountered it in about 1990.

THE RECORD I COULDN'T LIVE WITHOUT

Rachmaninov Piano Concerto No 3
Martha Argerich *pf* RSO Berlin / Riccardo Chailly
Philips/Decca
I love Martha Argerich's playing - the wildness of it, the humanity of it.

We used to have a bookshop in Old Brompton Road and there was a little music shop on the corner of South Kensington tube station, and I wandered in just beaming with happiness – I was in love, and had just got married – and I heard this music playing on the turntable. I just stood there and thought: 'What is this? It is beautiful.' Afterwards, I went up and asked the assistant what it was. I do play it a lot, I think it's absolutely breathtaking, particularly in the Perlman recording.

I've been going deaf for a number of years and am losing my top register more and more as the years go on, which means that I'm listening to music in a different way to everyone else. The other day I was driving along in the car, Classic FM was on, and they played *The Lark Ascending*. And of course there comes a portion when it just ascends into the stratosphere, so for me, my radio went completely silent. So I sang what I remembered of the work and a minute and a half later, back it came on for me – and I was exactly at the right note at the right time. It made me laugh very much! **G**

Samuel West

The actor in 2006 recalled his first Proms concert and explored the role of music in films

I was first taken to a Prom concert when I was six and contrary to all the things you are meant to do – make the first concert short, with lots of little movements to clap between – my mother took me to Handel's *Messiah*, most of which I slept through apparently, waking up and clapping very solemnly between acts. But like all children whose parents listen to music there were certain pieces that always excited me. *Young Person's Guide to the Orchestra* still thrills me, and *Carnival of the Animals*. Weirdly, the other work I remember is *Façade* (we had the Peter Pears/Edith Sitwell version) because I now perform it with my mother.

I learnt piano from the age of five and Suzuki cello from about seven. I had more fun with the cello because I enjoyed the togetherness of the orchestra, but I never became so good that I could play a different work according to my mood. I always dreamed of getting home from school, feeling melancholy and playing a melancholic piece or feeling excited and playing an exciting piece, but it always sounded the same.

When I was 17 I started working in the kitchens at the International Musicians' Seminar in Prussia Cove (now run by Steven Isserlis) because I wasn't good enough to play in the classes. To this day I still go and work in the kitchen. I stage-manage the odd concert and look after the music library sometimes, but mostly I do the washing up. I've discovered a lot of wonderful friends there.

I directed the English National Opera production of *Così fan tutte* in 2003 and would like to direct more opera in the future. Doing Gilbert & Sullivan in Sheffield would be fantastic because in Yorkshire there's a great oratorio and comic opera tradition. I like opera, but find it difficult sometimes to be absolutely certain it's the only mode in which the story can be told. Unless an opera is integrated musically and dramatically, which doesn't happen very often, I think, 'Why don't they just talk?' At times singers can be more interested in the effect of performance than in the intention of character. It seems to me that you sing something a particular way to express an idea. The need to speak and the need to sing are the same. So if you can direct singers like actors they generally understand what you mean. On the other hand, singers can give very concentrated performances because the physical effort of producing the sound makes them completely unselfconscious. As long as you can stop them trying to emote, what they are trying to say and the way they say it can be made to be the same.

I've worked with composers on three of the seven theatre productions I've directed and have always enjoyed the experience. The creative use of sound score in theatre needs to be more than covering scene changes, however, because music between scenes can make things seem very safe and conventional. Underscoring too I loathe in almost all cases. I remember a review of a performance by Judi Dench which

THE RECORD I COULDN'T LIVE WITHOUT

Mendelssohn Octet
Ensemble Explorations Harmonia Hundi
I'm taking a friend who doesn't like classical music to see the Mendelssohn Octet in Sheffield because I think it's impossible not to be dazzled by it. I find it rather frightening that he wrote it when he was 16 – devilish really.

said 'Her only soliloquy is touchingly underscored with cello'. I thought, 'I'm going to hate this production,' because one should either listen to cello or to Judi, but not both.

The first time I saw myself squashed by the bookcase in the film *Howard's End* there was no music and I remember being incredibly shocked by the silence. Of course the scene was never intended to be silent, but when I saw it with Richard Robbins's extraordinary soundtrack I wasn't sure it was better. I do sometimes think when actors are giving a very moving performance and a piano starts up they should complain, 'I'm sorry, can you stop? There's somebody playing a piano somewhere.' But they never do.

I've always loved Stravinsky, Kodály and Bartók and am a fan of most modern music. I keep pursuing the stuff even if it's difficult to listen to. If you go to a restaurant for ice cream and order what you feel like you get the nice, safe version, but if you say 'The chef knows more about ice cream than me, can he bring me something?' you may discover, 'My god, I never knew ice cream could be like this!' Sometimes it's frankly disgusting, but occasionally your ice cream horizons explode. There's no real possibility of that if you only go to things you're sure you'll like. The important thing, as Barenboim says, is 'always to listen in the hope you might actually hear', because listening does require attention and it's important to admit it's not always easy. But then the important things in life never are. **G**

Kevin Whately

The actor, talking in 2018, on his journey from folk to classical music, courtesy of his daughter, singer Kitty, and fellow actor John Thaw

Music was always in the house when I was growing up in the North East of England. My dad had a gramophone, and he'd play lots of folk music, like Owen Brannigan singing folk songs accompanied by Gerald Moore. My mum's collection was more classical – one of her favourites was Smetana's 'Vltava' from *Má vlast*, which I still have. Her mother, Doris Phillips, had trained as a soprano at the Royal College of Music in the 1900s. My grandfather was a self-made man from Newcastle and thought professional singers were the next worst thing to prostitutes, so it was only after he died that she pursued a singing career. She did quite a lot of BBC radio broadcasts, and sang at Newcastle City Hall.

We had a piano at home but I never learnt. My thing was singing folk songs and playing the guitar in pubs. I went with my friend Andy to Donegal for a year – we had a residency in a bar. When our tent got washed away, the owner, who had a chip shop around the back, cleared out all the potatoes from the stable and let us sleep there. This was 1969, when the Troubles were brewing, and we'd be singing rebel songs to the Irish. In hindsight, perhaps that wasn't such a good idea.

I would have been interested in pursuing folk music but when we got back I got side-tracked; I signed up to study accountancy, and then went to drama school. I don't really sing now; all my early theatre jobs involved singing (my professional debut was in Noël Coward's *Cowardy Custard*) but then the telly took over. I did *Gypsy* with Imelda Staunton at the Chichester Festival in 2014 though, and I sang with my niece Martha Tilson for a track on her folk album 'The Sea'.

When my daughter Kitty was born, my wife [the actress Madelaine Newton] and I would always sing to her. I can still remember her as a two-year-old, lying in her cot and singing to herself. In 1990, Madelaine and I were making a *Morse* episode, 'Masonic Mysteries', directed by Danny Boyle, which was based around *The Magic Flute*. We were using a cassette tape of Mozart's music for reference and after we'd finished filming, Danny gave it to me. Kitty latched on to it straight away – we would hear her trying out The Queen of the Night in her bedroom. The peripatetic music teachers here in Bedford were great – they picked her out and sent her for singing lessons at the RCM; later she went to Chetham's.

As Kitty's interest in singing grew, we started listening to more classical music. John Thaw was a huge classical music enthusiast, of course, and he'd talk to me about composers like Sibelius; I still enjoy listening to the symphonies, especially when I'm driving. I've never downloaded anything in my life – I like slotting a CD into the CD player in the car and being able to read the sleeve-notes. Opera possibly appeals to me more than orchestral music, probably because

THE RECORD I COULDN'T LIVE WITHOUT

Jonathan Dove Nights Not Spent Alone
Kitty Whately *mez* **Simon Lepper** *pf* Champs Hill
These Millay settings were initially suggested by my wife. The songs are gorgeous, and Kitty's recording has become staple night-time-driving listening.

it's so theatrical. The opera world couldn't be more different to the acting world. Kitty goes to Verbier, Aix … all these festivals heavily sponsored by huge international companies, while us actors potter about in places like East Acton. I know musicians are horribly underpaid, but they do get to play in wonderful places. Before she went to music college, Kitty sang in the chorus of *Giulio Cesare* at Glyndebourne and we went to see it. It was one of the best nights I've ever had.

The three of us – Kitty, my wife and I – often do concerts together. We've been performing pieces from Kitty's 2015 album 'This Other Eden', where we punctuate English songs with poetry readings by Hardy, Housman, and others. And later this year [2018], I'm the narrator in a production of *Candide* in Bergen with Kitty and her husband Anthony Gregory. In the past, I've narrated *Peter and the Wolf, Babar the Elephant* … I'm at an age where l like doing different things.

Appearing with the BBC Big Band for 'Our Finest Hour', which commemorates Dunkirk and the Battle of Britain, thrills me. It's like the Last Night of the Proms – it's that mixture of nostalgia and pride that resonates with people. There's music by Vera Lynn, Glenn Miller, Ron Goodwin – it's a really uplifting evening. Ⓖ
Kevin Whately supports SWAP'ra – Supporting Women and Parents in Opera (swap-ra.org)

Rowan Williams

The former Archbishop of Canterbury and Master of Magdalene College, Cambridge in 2016 on Britten, Bach and plainsong

I first became aware of classical music when I was a small boy, listening to the radio, and to bits of Tchaikovsky and Handel. But it was only in my teens that I started to listen harder, and probably around my middle teens when I started getting interested in early music. I can remember hearing Monteverdi's *Vespers* in the Guildhall in Swansea in about 1966. I was beginning to absorb a bit more Mozart, and can also remember mid- to late-teens developing a lasting passion for Britten, and deep devotion to Vaughan Williams as well.

Vaughan Williams is a supreme melodist – I loved his touch with folk song. When I first heard the *Five Variants of Dives and Lazarus*, that was like a casement window opening, as they say. Though I wrestled also with the slightly less cuddly aspects of Vaughan Williams in the symphonies.

I have a memory of listening on a very imperfect little transistor radio in my bedroom in 1966 to the first performance of Britten's *The Burning Fiery Furnace* from the Aldeburgh Festival. There was something about Britten's sharpness of edge mixed again with a tremendous melodic gift – but much more of the fingernail on the glass side, the wire in the blood – that gives you a sense of unease, which fascinated me. We performed *The Little Sweep* at school, and the church parables were being written in my late teens and I listened eagerly as they emerged. I discovered Britten's *Missa brevis* when I was about 16, and I still believe it is one of the great liturgical Masses of the 20th century.

I've always been fascinated by *The Turn of the Screw* as an opera. Britten really succeeds in making the flesh creep musically. It's a lot to do with how he shifts the focus on a key register very slightly up or down, and of course in one of the key parts pushing up the register so that discomfort is generated. It's a really complex, sophisticated and seriously alarming work. It puts you in touch with bits of the imagination that you'd rather not know about.

Bach remains for me the unsurpassable. In my 20s, looking back, it was a gradual unfolding of discovery from the Passions which I really learnt to know well as an undergraduate, through to more and more of the instrumental works and the cello suites particularly.

One of the things about Bach I find so compelling is that he will do the massed forces, and yet he can at the same time suggest with a single line any number of noises off, as it were. I've sometimes said of the cello suites that when you're listening to them you're left with an intense feeling that isn't a feeling about anything in particular. It's one of the things that makes listening to Bach – I know it's a cliché – like religious contemplation. It's not that you're feeling happy or

THE RECORD I COULDN'T LIVE WITHOUT

Bach Cello Suites

Paul Tortelier *vc* Warner Classics

It's not in every respect the performance that I think most apt but it's the first I got to know – I still think the exuberance of the performance is a rare gift.

feeling sad or anything – but you have just been participating in something that so stretches your insides.

I think plainsong is a very intelligent kind of music. It requires thought and feeling, both paced carefully and anchored carefully. They say in a lot of religious communities that you can tell something about the spiritual health of a community by the quality of the chant in the choir. Are people listening to each other, are they breathing together?

I find it interesting now to listen to recordings of early music that I heard back when the works were just being dusted off. Taverner's *Missa Corona Spinea*, one of my favourite works, I first heard on a cold evening in Merton College Chapel in Oxford in 1974 when the assessment of Tudor pitch was a great deal more ungenerous than it is today. In between the movements everybody just went off to rest for 10 minutes because it was so demanding! Whereas now it's a bit more realistic. Happily there are some good recordings, I've got a quite old recording from the early '70s and a more recent one by St Mary's Cathedral Edinburgh which is very nicely done. **G**

ILLUSTRATION: PHILIP BANNISTER

Bob Willis

The former England cricket captain revealed in 2007 – just before heading to the Ashes to commentate – about the eclectic selection of music on his iPod

I think for the Ashes tour my iPod's got about 775 Bob Dylan tracks, some 260 Van Morrison…and about 20 hours of Wagner!

My parents, who introduced me to classical music as a young teenager, were pretty keen on Beethoven. Then at school, in the '60s, I was labelled a bit of a rebel, so I got into Mahler and Shostakovich and used to hear them at the Festival Hall. My classical collection was fairly mainstream – Beethoven symphonies and your Mozart. I got into opera later and it was around 1980 that I got stung by Richard Wagner. I was on a trip in Vienna and the choice of entertainment on the Saturday evening was either a bierkeller or the Staatsoper.

A friend and I decided to do the thing in style, take our dinner jackets and go to the opera, which happened to be *Die Meistersinger*. A neighbour gave me a bit of a tutorial and I was captivated immediately. Wagner takes a lot of studying and I spent an enormous amount of time in the 1980s and '90s listening to his music.

The *Ring* and *Parsifal* became my favourites … If I had to rate them, I suppose *Parsifal*, *Götterdämmerung* and *Die Walküre* would be my top three. I went to a complete *Ring* cycle in Adelaide during the 1998/99 Ashes tour, with an international cast conducted by Jeffrey Tate with the Adelaide Symphony Orchestra. I was commentating for Sky, but my boss let me go early one day for a 4.30 start. I didn't miss too much of the cricket, but we've got to get our priorities right!

Music has always been really important on tour but, once I had discovered Wagner, most other operas sort of disappeared into the background and I don't really listen to anything much in the popular music field apart from Van Morrison and Dylan, so these three have filled a vast amount of time.

It's true I get a little fanatical about things – and, yes, I did adopt Dylan's name as well – so I probably tend to miss out and ignore other excellent pieces.

I go to quite a lot of music with Michael Henderson, who writes about both cricket and music. We go up to the Edinburgh Festival when it isn't clashing with cricket and we've been to Paris to see *Parsifal*. We also went to the semi-staged *Ring* at the Royal Albert Hall and we've been to all four parts of the *Ring* over a period of years.

I don't much care for the current Covent Garden *Ring*, though. I didn't like the production at all and John Treleaven is not one of my favourite Siegfrieds.

INTERVIEW BY ANTONY CRAIG ILLUSTRATION: BRIAN GALLAGHER

THE RECORD I COULDN'T LIVE WITHOUT

Wagner Götterdämmerung
Soloists; ENO / Sir Reginald Goodall
Chandos
Brünnhilde's immolation from Götterdämmerung. It makes me cry, if the audience don't start their ridiculous bloody applause before the final note's played. Those strings at the end of Götterdämmerung just wrench your soul out. I prefer the live Reginald Goodall ENO Twilight of the Gods from 1977 with Rita Hunter as Brünnhilde.

I think *Parsifal* is my overall favourite because, although I'm not a religious person, I find the music – the first act in particular – just so moving … the transformation scenes, the beautiful choral stuff, when Gurnemanz is introducing Parsifal to the knights and so on. I think that's the most beautiful music ever written.

Being captain of England can be quite a solitary existence in some ways, when you have come out of the ranks of being one of the lads. One of my tours was to Pakistan. There's not a lot of entertainment there and no bars to congregate in, anyway, and this was before the days of DVD and stuff which the guys would now watch, so I'd go and listen to music quite happily on my own, occasionally on headphones but usually on a cassette player.

I always liked Shostakovich 8 to get the blood running – the start of the third movement … the trumpets, trombones and drums – pretty stirring stuff. To wind down I love Mahler 4. And English music away from home helps a lot … Delius and Vaughan Williams – *The Lark Ascending*, *First Cuckoo in Spring*. That sort of stuff. Not quite *Jerusalem* and *Land of Hope and Glory*, but on the road to that I suppose.

I don't play any music myself. I don't have any classical training in singing, either. I don't have the patience to practise, I'm afraid. Actually, I never had the patience to practise my cricket, so practising the Spanish guitar my parents kindly got me for Christmas when I was 14 was just too much bother. **G**

AN Wilson

In 2005 the author shared with us his love
of music for the church and works by Wagner

My father had a wind-up gramophone on which he used to play Rachmaninov piano concertos and César Franck. But he was quite an old dad, and by the time I'd come along as the last child he would not let me learn an instrument. So my musical education really began with those old records that he'd collected but had stopped listening to.

I was in a choir at school, and it's one of the most formative things that happened to me, even though I didn't realise it at the time. We sang Haydn's *Creation* and *Seasons*, Mendelssohn's *Elijah*, things like that. You learn so much.

The choral tradition in England is astounding. I know it's not as advanced as it is in Germany, let's say, but the extraordinary thing about it is it's still universal in England. Although the choir schools and the cathedrals have been bled to death financially there are still these extraordinary, quite small places which produce paid choirs singing this music. In England you can more or less take it for granted that if you're in a cathedral city or a town with a big church that you'll hear a wonderful rendition of the Mass on a Sunday. We're very, very lucky.

I don't think it's an accident that religion – many, many religions – is so often communicated musically. The Gospels almost certainly began by being chanted, just as in the Buddhist tradition the stories told by the great religious masters are sung. There's a kind of rhythm of life heard behind it all. When you hear the Passion sung on Palm Sunday, you really do feel you're in touch with something very, very ancient indeed, in terms of a human tradition.

I feel that my own changes through life and education in the broadest sense are reflected in my much, much wider understanding of music now. If you'd asked me when I was in my 20s, I'd have said I mainly like English music: Purcell, English church music (the Anglican settings of the psalms are still my favourite church music), Elgar, and, for light relief, Noël Coward songs. Whereas now I think the great giants are Bach, Beethoven and Wagner.

At Rugby School there was a big concert hall which was also used by the town. Janet Baker came with the Birmingham Symphony Orchestra and our school choir joined forces with the local Rugby choir, and we sang our way through *The Dream of Gerontius*. In those days I'd never heard a Wagner opera so what I was falling in love with was *Parsifal* really. I do think *The Dream of Gerontius* is a fantastic work, but it is basically a kind of homage to *Parsifal*, and I hadn't the first idea about that then.

For a very long time I was resistant to Wagner – I thought I could not sit in a theatre for five hours. But then I saw *Tristan*, and it opened my ears and eyes to his music. There's so much going on in the music. Wagner is the first composer that I know

THE RECORD I COULDN'T LIVE WITHOUT

Wagner Die Walküre
Soloists; Vienna PO / Sir Georg Solti
Decca
I think the last act of *Die Walküre* is the best bit of Wagner – I play it practically every day.

about who is also a would-be poet, a would-be philosopher. One of the interesting aspects about the whole thing musically and philosophically is that he composed the libretto to *The Ring* first, and then fundamentally change his attitude to life while composing the music. There's a fantastic tension which is what really makes it so exciting: between the fundamentalism of the young Hegelian, revolutionary Wagner who wrote the libretto, who just thought, basically, God was dead, a new world had come into being – and then this Schopenhauerian mystic who actually writes the music.

He had such an absorbent intelligence. He seemed to be aware of why people were losing their faith in Europe, what science was going to bring to the human race, the kind of destruction that would come as a result of industrialisation and changes in political powers; there's a philosophical, musical and aesthetic entirety.

Music helped a great deal with writing *The Victorians*, my book about the period. I played it all the time, particularly *The Ring*. Before that I wrote a book called *God's Funeral* about the decline of faith in the 19th century. I felt that actually the most intelligent thing ever written or composed on that subject was not books like mine from the 20th-century perspective, and not either Cardinal Newman trying to defend religion or Herbert Spencer and co trying to attack it, but it was Wagner. He'd really seen the emotional impact of it all. If you want to feel what it's like to be a churned-up, crazy, mixed-up Victorian about all these things – and about capitalism and social change, too – then it's all in *The Ring*. ⓖ

ILLUSTRATION: NEALE OSBORNE

Brian Wilson

One of the most influential songwriters of the 20th century, Beach Boy Brian Wilson, revealed to us in 2011 the music that has inspired his unique sound world

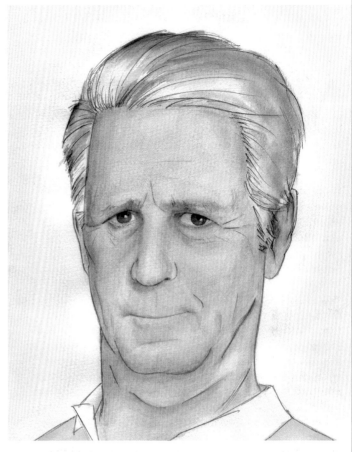

The first piece of music I ever heard was George Gershwin's *Rhapsody in Blue*. My grandmother and mother played it for me at my grandmother's house. They laid me down on the floor by the record player and they put *Rhapsody in Blue* on. I was too young to say 'Oh, mum I love this music!' but I just took it in – and it blew my mind! And later on in my life, when I was 28, I listened a lot to Leonard Bernstein's version and I learnt how to play the main theme by ear, sitting at the piano.

As a musician I am completely self-taught. When I was growing up I listened to a great deal of Bach and Tchaikovsky – that was my musical education. I never even sang in a choir at school, I taught myself to sing. These days I don't listen to current music, I listen to oldies-but-goodies: Diana Ross, Marvin Gaye, Elton John, Paul McCartney, The Doors, The Who, The Rolling Stones, The Bee Gees, those sorts of groups.

So Gershwin was my first love. My second was the Four Freshmen and then after that, believe it or not, Phil Spector for his unbelievable record production. Those three things combined in my own sound. The sound I became known for in the 1960s came from the music in the 1950s, the harmonies of the Four Freshman, Rosemary Clooney, who taught me a lot about phrasing and how to sing sweetly and gently, and Chuck Berry, who taught me how to write rock'n'roll melodies. I was filled to the brim with musical education from listening to these artists.

People have said that some of my songs (particularly *Good Vibrations*) sound like classical compositions but I don't agree. At the time I just wanted to write music in a modern and current way. The truth about *Good Vibrations* is that I was challenged to write a song to match *You've lost that lovin' feeling*. I heard that record and I said to myself, 'I've got to make a record that good!' We recorded *Good Vibrations* in five different studios. At the last studio session (at RCA Victor) we did the vocal tracks. The night we did the vocals the guys in the studio said, 'Brian, this is going to be a Number One record'. I said, 'I know, I know!' It was a really great feeling. We knew immediately that we had a Number One record on our hands. When I look back at my career the songs I'm most proud of are *California Girls*, *Don't Worry Baby*, *Good Vibrations* and *God Only Knows*.

I still enjoy performing live. I'm getting a little older these days so it's getting a little harder to perform, but I still like to do it.

THE RECORD I COULDN'T LIVE WITHOUT

Gershwin Rhapsody in Blue
Leonard Bernstein Sony Classical
I have loved *Rhapsody in Blue* all my life, and I still think that this Leonard Bernstein recording is the best.

My latest album is a collection of Gershwin songs called 'Brian Wilson Reimagines Gershwin'. I wanted to present Gershwin to the people of today so that they could appreciate where his music was at. So I took each song and treated it separately, the way it should be sung, the way Gerhswin would have wanted it to be sung. My orchestrator, Paul Mertons, lined up 25 Ira and George Gershwin songs and we narrowed it down from 25 to 12 altogether. Then we learnt each song separately in the studio. Believe it or not, the Disney people sent me over 104 unfinished Gershwin songs that George himself played on the piano and they asked us to choose just two of those songs to complete and write new songs around. Those songs became *Nuttin' but love* and *The like in I love you*.

Fifteen years ago I started listening to a lot of Bach again. I have found his music to be very therapeutic for me, something that has never left my side. Ⓖ
'Brian Wilson Reimagines Gershwin' is available on the Disney Pearl label.

Jeanette Winterson

The author talked to us in 2009 about the need to find total abandonment in music

My mother, who played the piano by ear, used to bang out Kathleen Ferrier songs. Ferrier was a great heroine of hers, being a fellow Blackburn girl. To this day I love that old contralto sound. It's fascinating to hear how voices have changed between now and then, between Kathleen Ferrier and Sarah Connolly.

So, it was Mrs Winterson pounding 'What is life to me without thee' on her old upright piano that was my first experience of music. I wasn't allowed to learn to play the piano because my mother did and she fantasised that we might play duets one day. So I had to learn the violin, which I hated. Scraping away at the fiddle was a mistake and set my love of music back.

But I went to a grammar school for girls where I had a marvellous music teacher who also played cello in the Hallé Orchestra. She had high ambitions for my classmates and I. We had to put on the Fauré Requiem for our Christmas concert – no small feat! And it was quite something. Teaching music at that level was unusual and we all, I am sure, benefited. Now the situation in schools is much worse. Kids love music. They have a natural instinct for it just as they have that natural instinct for story-telling. Creativity is there, born in every child. Then we breed it out of them by calling culture elitism and that is monstrous. In teaching music in schools nothing is forced upon children. In taking away that teaching we take away something that is theirs by right.

I would never be without music now. There is a link there with my work as a writer. If you're a very verbal person and work with words, you should be able to go to music and immediately engage with an emotional experience. When I listen, I don't analyse it or think about it, I am, simply, in it. There is a totality of experience there. You can abandon yourself to it without questioning. In that it is like sex. In life, we're always trying to tear things apart and analyse them and that isn't always helpful. The therapeutic value of music is very great. It returns us to a state of feeling that is very rare.

I don't separate music and indeed all the other arts from what I do. I live in a creative continuum which includes music very naturally. It is simply a part of my life in the same way that language is. Except that the non-verbal component is very important. That's why I can't bear surtitles at the opera. Anybody can work out what's happening before they go in just by reading up on the story! If you're constantly looking up at the surtitles you're keeping the left side of your brain switched on in the way you simply cannot in a concert because there are often no words. People don't let themselves go at the opera as they should. If you keep that left side of your brain on then you're being allowed to stay in your own world, to be comfortable. Opera is not about being

THE RECORD I COULDN'T LIVE WITHOUT

Wagner Der Ring des Nibelungen
Soloists; Bayreuth Festival / Daniel Barenboim
Warner Classics
This cycle is so massive, you can live inside it for a long time with plenty still to discover.

comfortable, it's about surrendering. Language helps you stay in your own little world – which is why people read books on the bus. Music lets you open up.

So when done properly, I am a huge opera fan. I have a rule that if I don't know an opera I see it in performance first and follow that up by listening to a recording. I rarely get the thing on the first go – recently I had an interesting experience with Britten's *Death in Venice* where I went to see it twice and felt shut out both times. I was in despair, until I heard it on the radio and suddenly, at the third listening, it made complete sense. I heard what the music was doing. It had taken me three goes to be inside it. That was a lesson for me. We give up too easily with classical music, especially modern music.

I have my places and companies that I love – like Glyndebourne and ENO. And there are performers whom I particularly admire. I love Natalie Clein's playing and talking to her about music gives you so many insights. Ultimately though, it's not about heroes for me, it's about finding new places. **G**

'Midsummer Nights' – stories inspired by opera – is edited by Jeanette Winterson

Lucy Worsley

The historian, writer and chief curator at Historic Royal Palaces spoke in 2012 about how music can help bring history to life

I first encountered classical music when my grandad gave us a piano and I started to have lessons when I was four. I didn't realise it was classical music then. I live in a flat now but if I visit somebody who has a piano I fall on it like a ravening beast. If you had lessons for 15 years, as I did – I did all my grades – it's bound to have a really deep effect on your life.

My piano teacher Miss Beaumont taught me for those 15 years. At the time I was terrified of her but in retrospect she gave me a great gift of self-discipline and self-reliance. She made me strive for excellence and work hard. To help somebody to get better and really to challenge them, that's a rare and valuable thing. That's true of music and performance but also of any other part of life, really.

My piano-playing came to a sad end. This was the worst day of my life so far – and I'm afraid that tells you an awful lot about me. In 1992 Labour lost the election and I was devastated by this, because I was quite a leftie at the time. Secondly, the pupils lost the pupils vs teachers quiz at our school, and I really thought we were going to win. And thirdly, the news came that I had failed my Trinity College piano diploma, and I thought I was going to pass. It all happened on the same day. It was the perfect storm of bad news for me, aged 18 or whatever I was. That was the end of my officially competitive, serious piano-playing. After that I did go on for a while by myself playing things that I really wanted to play and hadn't been allowed to before, because when I was having my lessons I always had to play Mozart – so I played Chopin and Liszt, and that sort of thing. I went off the straight and narrow.

The reason I stopped playing at university was that I couldn't afford lessons any more and, to play, we had to go the porter's lodge and get a special key, so that was an obstacle. I went to New College, Oxford – I remember once trying to persuade Edward Higginbottom that when he took the choristers on a tour of Australia he really needed to take some nannies, which was going to be me and my friends, but he said no.

I also play the clarinet – that's my second instrument. My third instrument is the tenor saxophone and I used to play in the band when I was at school. The reason I went for that one is that I felt I'd become chained to the printed page of my piano music. I've never been very good at improvisation but it forced me to do it.

We haven't succeeded in doing this yet but we want to get someone to do a PhD in the music played in all the different rooms at different times at Kensington Palace and Hampton Court Palace. We're looking for funding – it's just such a perfect project for somebody – and then we could play the music in the rooms. We recently had a big conference at Kensington Palace, and Oliver Davies, a retired professor f

THE RECORD I COULDN'T LIVE WITHOUT

Czerny Fantasia on Favourite Motifs from I Puritani
Thomas Fischer *pf* Naxos
This was one of the teenage Victoria's favourite operas. She often played arrangements on the piano at home, sometimes as duets with her half-sister or mother.

rom the Royal College of Music, put together a special concert programme to entertain us in the evening. It was all music that had either been written for, or dedicated to, or had been played by all the people who lived at Kensington Palace. To hear the music that the young Victoria could well have played, in the very rooms where she might have played it, was remarkable. To my mind, it brought this romantic, rebellious but rather repressed teenager to life.

Queen Victoria's mother, Queen Victoria and Albert and their daughters had very high standards and they were very, very good amateur musicians – I suppose they could afford good lessons and spent their time playing with professional musicians; and of course music was much more part of the fabric, the warp and weft of daily life then. Even though she was running the country to a certain extent, practically every day Queen Victoria would set aside half an hour and she and Albert would play together. When he died, one of the signifiers that she wasn't well, that she was in mourning, was that she stopped playing. And one of the signs that she was coming back to life again, 10 years or so later, was that she started playing and listening to music once again. **G**

Victoria Wood

The late comedian, actor, director and playwright in 2013 on the need for music education and her love of choirs

Classical music is a big presence in my life; I listen to it all the time. I did O level and A level Music and, of course, I've been exposed to much more since then. My piano-playing these days, though, is minimal and sporadic. I can read music, I can play, and I think having some kind of musicality absolutely helps with comic writing. Everything you write has to have a rhythm and that's why I always ask people to stick to the lines I've written and not rewrite them, because I hear them in my head and they have to deliver a certain 'oomph'. So it all comes back to music. If you're doing voices, there's a musicality there.

Jokes work only when they're done to a certain rhythm, and when you meet someone who can't tell a joke it's usually because they've got no sense of rhythm. In the past I've had a group of people I've worked with regularly, and as we all have our own way of working it's more fun when you find those who work your way.

I do go to concerts but the bulk of my listening is from the radio and CDs. I find the concert experience quite a chilly environment and really get irritated with women orchestral players coming on and putting their handbags down by the side of the chair – there's no theatricality there at all! I think it would be so much better if they all came on together and sat down at the same time instead of chatting, putting their hair-slides in and tugging at their cardigans. If you're going to do that then put a curtain down and then raise it when they're ready to start. We've paid to see something and I expect more. There's no respect for the audience in the way that a concert starts and the way that a conductor comes on silently. Why not come on and say, 'Hello, this is what we're going to play,' and maybe tell us a tiny bit about it, and *then* get going? It seems we're almost excluded as audience members. Also, I'm not good at sitting still. I always want to get up and walk about. So I suppose I really do prefer listening at home.

Both my kids are musical: one's training to be an opera singer and the other one works for a music producer, so music is their life, really. I didn't push it, but it was always something we did together. We'd sit and sing songs, and I'd make up songs at the piano for them. And they both played instruments when they were little.

I think it's a big problem if the only people who have access to music lessons are middle-class. It's the same with acting – if the only people who can afford to train are middle-class people then that's a shocking thought. We just won't continue to have the theatrical heritage that we've had up till now.

THE RECORD I COULDN'T LIVE WITHOUT

Bach Advent Cantatas, BWV36, 61 and 62
Soloists; Monteverdi Choir; English Baroque Soloists / Sir John Eliot Gardiner
Archiv
Because of my daughter, I've become increasingly drawn to choral music. I love voices, and I love Bach.

At the moment I'm more drawn to choral music, because my daughter was a choral scholar at Cambridge and I was exposed to a lot of her work. And I love Bach – I'm listening to all the Advent cantatas in the kitchen. I love voices – and I also love brass.

I suppose I love ensemble music, too … I used to play the trumpet in a military band. It's very special making music in a group and I love that there's a real buzz about choirs going on at the moment. I wrote a musical about a choir that was put on in Manchester a couple of years ago – it was about a children's choir recording *Nymphs and Shepherds* and was set in 1929. As I say, choirs are very 'in' right now, and it's great for people when they can just sing in a group. There's something wonderful about it – the physicality, making a noise together. It does an awful lot for you, singing with other people. **G**

Franco Zeffirelli

The Italian director of film, play and opera, who died in 2019, recalled in 2005 the extraordinary gifts of Callas and Karajan

Long before I dreamed of becoming an actor I was a fan of music. We often went to the opera when I was eight, nine and ten. I remember the first opera I saw was Wagner's *Walküre* in Florence because the baritone who sang Wotan was a friend of my uncle. I was so fascinated by the miracle of opera; I was really imbued with it since childhood.

I came to Rome when Luchino Visconti auditioned me as an actor to work in his company. Then I got the leading young role in the Anna Magnani film *L'Onorevole Angelina*. They were offering me several propositions but Visconti was preparing his first film after the war, *La terra trema*, and I went to work with him as assistant director. And I carried on, although having always an eye on music and opera. I made my debut in La Scala in 1954 with *L'italiana in Algeri* sung by Giulietta Simionato and conducted by Carlo Maria Giulini. I didn't expect it but it happened because I was the scene designer for Visconti. For quite a while my work was only in the opera theatre.

I heard Maria Callas for the first time in Rome as Kundry in *Parsifal* – I was working then for Visconti in the theatre as production designer/manager assisting Salvador Dalí. She was certainly one of the top, absolute talents. And in Rome she was a sensation: I became her fan instantly. Fat – almost obese! – but the voice could not be forgotten. So later I followed her wherever she was performing.

She was a combination of many perfections. She was an educated lady – the diction and the way she matched the singing voice with the words was unique. Then she had a very special voice, a combination of two completely different voices. She could sing anything in those years. In fact, she did. Reality is a very hard word to define: Callas managed to be absolutely real and believe in her character so much when she was performing that she forgot it was all an artifice. Only extreme professional effort gives you the illusion of total reality.

I've had three different careers, three lives: theatre, film and opera. One film where all three met together was *Otello* with Plácido Domingo. That for me is the ultimate of my successes. I put all the immense treasure that was offered me into a new form of art.

In the early days I worked alongside Herbert von Karajan who was very whimsical, a great 'star'. He was aware of everything he did and said, but when someone is so famous, is a *divo*, like him, the basis of their success must be absolute superior competence, professional competence. Am I a *divo*? No, not at all. I am very successful. My name is a guarantee. I have never disappointed those who set their heart on my work. I have never delivered a big flop where I got everything wrong. But I don't think I'm a *divo*.

INTERVIEW BY CHARLES SEARSON ILLUSTRATION: DANIEL MACKIE

THE RECORD I COULDN'T LIVE WITHOUT

Puccini Tosca
Soloists; La Scala / Victor de Sabata
Warner Classics
The recording I play most of all is the Tosca of De Sabata with Callas and Tito Gobbi. The ultimate perfection.

If we talk about recent events at La Scala, the mistake that Riccardo Muti made was to do 19 consecutive opening nights of the season. Last year's choice of Salieri's *L'Europa riconosciuta* – the work with which the theatre first opened in 1778 – was a total bore, a waste of money. When I made my debut Victor de Sabata was the general artistic manager but he did not impose himself on all the opening nights. There was Karajan, there was Furtwängler, Votto, Gavazzeni, Giulini, other conductors. You cannot judge the present season at La Scala because it's the heritage of the people before. I know Stéphane Lissner, the new head, is a wonderful man. He begins his personal approach to programming next season, and I think I'm going to go back to La Scala with a new production to open the season.

At the moment I'm listening to *Aida* because I am beginning rehearsals in Moscow for it. My head is full of *Aida*, which I've done 100 times but every time is a new revelation. **G**

Hans Zimmer

Back in 2010, the composer reflected on how he writes music for the cinema

When I was a boy, my parents didn't have a television but they did have a piano, and as far back as I can remember I would torture that poor piano, making horrific noises. It was more fun than anything else and it certainly kept me out of trouble. Then, when I was roughly 12 years old, I sneaked into my local cinema to see *Once Upon a Time in the West*. I remember thinking, 'This is what I want to do,' but of course, as a kid living in the country in Germany, getting to Hollywood was much more difficult than simply buying a plane ticket.

Later I was in a band and we had a hit, but I just loathed it. If you have ever seen *Spinal Tap*, the whole band experience is just like that. So I realised that wasn't the life for me and I became an assistant to a film composer called Stanley Myers. He knew everything about the orchestra but nothing about electronics. I, on the other hand, knew a lot about electronics and nothing about the orchestra. So – in exchange for me figuring out how to work his espresso machine – he taught me about the orchestra. From the start he was very collaborative. I was never a ghost writer and after a while I was assigned movies of my own.

I happened to write the score for a small British movie called *A World Apart*, which was brought to the attention of Barry Levinson, who had just made *Good Morning Vietnam*. He didn't have my phone number but somehow had the address for my studio in London. One evening, at around 11 o'clock, my doorbell rang and there was this guy standing there. He said, 'Hi, I'm Barry Levinson, I'm a Hollywood director. Would you like to do a Hollywood movie?' And that was it!

When I am scoring a film I ask myself, what is the tone of the story and what is the point of view? I tend to procrastinate for ever but eventually I have to sit down and write a theme. This never comes easily and there is always a lot of despair involved, a lot of, 'I don't think I can do this again. I need to tell them to hire somebody decent'. A bus driver will get better at his route with experience but I am supposed to start with a clean slate each time, and because I have written so many soundtracks avoiding repetition is difficult. Sequels are very interesting in this respect. When composing for *The Dark Knight*, I tried to pretend *Batman Begins* didn't exist, literally starting from scratch. Then, whenever there were gaps, there was always material from the first film to fall back on.

I rarely see the film before I start writing and often I don't read the script because I much prefer to have a conversation with the director. Then I know what movie he is making in his head, and of course, each one has very specific requirements. I am about to start working with Chris Nolan again and am also working with James Brooks, who directed *As Good as it Gets*. They are very different personalities so the

THE RECORD I COULDN'T LIVE WITHOUT

Mozart *Ave verum corpus*
Concentus Musicus Wien / Nikolaus Harnoncourt
Warner Classics
Mozart's *Ave verum corpus* is 40 bars of sheer perfection.

music performs contrasting roles in their films. Working with Guy Ritchie on *Sherlock Holmes* was different again. Guy is a very physical director and would actually conduct me at the piano.

Music in Hollywood has changed a great deal. There used to be an army of orchestrators, arrangers and copiers employed by the studio – André Previn was part of one of those vast music departments. These days those divisions have fallen by the wayside. I write on a computer, which allows me to be very specific about the nuance of every note, much more so than writing on paper. But you do miss that terrific focused emotion of a group of musicians playing together. So I like to collaborate with other composers and musicians because it allows me to capture that sense of teamwork.

There are many classical composers that I love. Bach is forever my teacher and I listen to him constantly. I also love Mozart, Brahms and all the Schubert Lieder. In my studio I have enormous speakers – double the size of whatever you think of as 'large' – and one night we put on this incredible Bernstein performance of Mahler's Second and just cranked it up. It was a great evening and we all went home very humbled. **G**